POSTAL TEST 473E
SPEED-STUDY GUIDE

Angelo Tropea

ISBN-13: 978-1517494322

ISBN-10: 151749432X

Published by Angelo Tropea Books, Inc.

Please note that the addresses and forms in this book are fictitious and are presented for instructional purposes only.

"The will to win, the desire to succeed, the urge to reach your full potential... these are the keys that will unlock the door to personal excellence."

-Confucius

CONTENTS

Practice Tests

INTRODUCTION

You must score well on the Postal Test 473E to be considered for appointment.

Because of this, the aim of this book is to **keep it simple – and focused** on the actual test instead of complicating it with other information about the postal service and government jobs which does not contribute to attaining a higher score on the test.

The postal service has improved the process for applying and testing for certain postal positions. Generally, the application and testing process for the postal positions covered by this book has been computerized, as follows:

eCareers (Online application system)

Candidates for the following career postal positions who are required to take the new postal exam 473E (which has replaced the old 460 and 473 series of exams) now apply online at the USPS website:

http://www.usps.com/employment/

These postal positions are:

1. CITY CARRIER

(Applicants must have a current valid state driver's license, at least two years of documented driving experience, and a safe driving record.)

City carriers deliver and collect mail outdoors and may carry a full mail bag up to 35 pounds on their shoulders. They also may be required to load and unload trays and containers and parcels up to 70 pounds.

2. MAIL PROCESSING CLERK

Employees who are mail processing clerks work with and monitor automated mail processing equipment and sometimes have to lift or transport containers that may be heavy.

3. MAIL HANDLER

Mail handlers transport mail within buildings and may have to lift and carry containers up to 70 pounds and push rolling containers within buildings.

4. SALES, SERVICES, AND DISTRIBUTION ASSOCIATE

Persons selected to be associates must successfully complete a job training program. Associates provide customer support, including in direct sales. They may also work distributing the mail.

5. RURAL CARRIER ASSOCIATE

Initially work less than a full week (part-time) and are not initially career employees.   They work on a call-in basis and based on seniority may be offered a career rural carrier associate job when one becomes available.

With eCareers candidates may apply AT ANY TIME and may apply for jobs in ANY STATE (nationwide).

In addition to career positions which require you to do well on the computerized exam 473E, you may also apply online for part-time or temporary jobs not requiring taking exam 473E.

To apply, you may follow these instructions:

1. Go to the website   **http://www.usps.com/employment/**

First click on "Create An Account" which is found in the box on the right side of the web page. The process of creating your profile is explained in each screen. We suggest that you read carefully the requirements of each screen and answer appropriately.

The Account will be used by the online system to fill in automatically your information whenever you apply online for a postal position. The system will require you to create a "User Name" and "Password" and will also ask you for your e-mail address so that the postal service will be able to communicate with you.

2. Return to the website   **http://www.usps.com/employment/**

In the "Search Open Jobs" section on the right side of the screen, click the "Search Now" button. That will take you to the "Job Search" screen. If you wish to search for any open "City Carrier" positions, for example, you would type 'City Carrier' in the "Full Text Search, Keywords" box and then select the "Search Criteria for Employment Opportunities" which may be a City (for example New York City), OR a LOCATION (for example, Alabama), OR a ZIP code (example 11201)

A screen showing "Search result" will appear. This screen will have a list of available positions in the area that you selected. To apply for a position click on the line which lists that position. This will cause a screen to appear which lists the details of that position. The positions covered by this book require that you take postal exam 473E. Other positions (temporary positions, casual positions) may not require an exam.

The 473E exam is comprised of 2 parts:

Part 1:

A "Personal Characteristics and Experience Inventory" test which you take using the computer. This test is used to determine the suitability of candidates. Candidates usually take this test on their computer (or a computer in a library, or other facility where computers are available). This section of the test is explained further in this book. Candidates who pass this section of the test are notified to take Part 2 of the test in a supervised testing facility.

Part 2:

A supervised testing facility is a place where there are a number of computers and where candidates take the test 473E simultaneously under supervision of postal representatives. Part 2 of the postal 473E has questions on the following areas:

1. Address Checking
2. Forms completion
3. Coding of addresses (by **referring** to a coding chart)
4. Coding of addresses (by **memory** of same coding chart in section 3, above)

All of these types of questions are explained in this book.

Although the 473E is administered using a computer at a testing facility, we believe strongly that in order to prepare for this exam it is wise to become completely familiar with the different types of questions that are asked and also to practice them with a book BEFORE you attempt to take any online practice versions of the test. The purpose of this book is to help transition you to the computer exam by taking away any uncertainty you may have regarding the exam content and test taking strategy.

To help you visualize an online format of the questions on the 473E test, we have provided a web site with sample online test questions. These sample questions are available for free at **http://www.postaltest.com**

An interactive version of the questions is available for those with an Access Code
(See bottom of page 63 for FREE INTERACTIVE Access Code)

This book and online sample test questions are designed to focus on the TEST.

There are other good books on the market which focus on job descriptions, benefits, etc. You may also obtain all that information for free at the USPS web site at:

http://www.usps.com/employment

The information provided by the USPS is professional and complete.

Our aim is not to repeat what the USPS already says well, but to provide additional exercises and explanations and hints about the types of questions that are asked with the aim of enhancing your grade and thereby increasing your chances of being offered a job.

Among the topics covered at the USPS web site under the "Careers" tab are:

1. Delivery & Operations
2. Corporate
3. Students & Graduates
4. Transitioning Military
5. Workin at UPS
6. Search and Apply

Other Eligibility Requirements

In addition to the requirements listed below, the employment history of applicants is reviewed. Their military history is reviewed, if applicable, and a criminal records check is also made. Ability to lift packages is also assessed.

Age:

1. (with a high school diploma) must be at least 16 at time of appointment.
2. (without a high school diploma) must be at least 18 at time of appointment.

Citizenship:

1. U.S. citizen, or
2. permanent resident alien, or citizen of American Samoa or other U.S. territory.

English skills:

Must have basic English competency

Drug test and Medical Assessment:

A urinalysis drug screening will be conducted and a Medical Assessment is made.

Driving record:

For jobs requiring driving, like City Carrier, the driving record will be reviewed.

Selective Service:

Males born after 12/31/59 must be registered with Selective Service at age 18.

(Please visit the USPS web site for full details.)

We believe that the combination of this book, the sample questions available **FREE** online, and a careful review and submission of job requests (at the postal web site: http://www.usps.com/employment) will greatly enhance your chances of success.

What will improve your chances even more are hard work and your desire to succeed.

The Postal Test 473E

The test consists of 5 timed parts:

1. Address Checking

2. Forms Completion

3. Coding

4. Memory

5. Personal Characteristics and Experience Inventory

Part	Time Allowed	Number of Ques.	Description of Question
1. Address Checking	11 minutes	60	Compare two addresses
2. Forms Completion	15 minutes	30	Correctly complete forms
3. Coding	6 minutes	36	Find correct code for address
4. Memory (of coding examples, above)	7 minutes	36	Memorize address codes (which are same as codes in "Coding" section part of the test.)
5. Personal Characteristics and Experience Inventory	90 minutes	236	Tests for experience and job-related tendencies

Total "Time Allowed" for Parts 1-4 is 39 minutes.

HOW TO USE THIS BOOK

If I escorted you and a group of other people to the front of a beautiful house and announced that the house would be awarded to the first person who opens the front door, there probably would be a mad rush for that door.

Of course, if the door were unlocked, the fastest runner would probably win the house. However, if the door were locked, then the person with the KEY - even if he or she was not the fastest person - would win the house.

What I am trying to stress is the following:

1. Do NOT be a part of the crowd of other applicants who runs into the test unprepared.

2. Practice with this book and online sample questions diligently so that you will have the "KEY" to achieving a successful score.

3. You don't have to be the most intelligent or educated person to be the highest scorer.

To prepare for the test, do the following:

1. Read carefully the descriptions of the different sections of the test.

2. Study carefully the HINTS in the sections and also for the test-taking section.

3. Do the exercises for each of the sections.

4. When you think you are ready, take all of the 7 Practice Tests and review the online test questions samples (See page 83 for PostelTest.com Access Code).

You will be surprised at how much better you will do!

If you find that you need motivation, consider the following quote:

"Always bear in mind that your resolution to succeed is more important than any (other) thing."
- Abraham Lincoln

ADDRESS CHECKING

Comparing two addresses (Street number, City, State, and Zip) should be easy, but it is not as easy as it first appears. The reason is that this section of the test measures your ability to work BOTH QUICKLY AND ACCURATELY.

You are provided with 60 pairs of addresses which you must compare and decide whether:

  A. There are no errors (differences) in the addresses: "NO ERRORS"

  B. There is an error (difference) in the address only: "ADDRESS ONLY"

  C. There is an error (difference) in the ZIP code only: "ZIP CODE ONLY"

  D. There are errors (differences) in both the address and ZIP: "BOTH"

To accomplish this, you are allotted a maximum of 11 minutes (5-6 addresses per minute).

This is a reasonable amount of time. Even if at first you find the time limit difficult, with practice you should be able to comfortably complete the 60 comparisons within the allotted time.

7 HINTS for Success

Addresses are composed of numbers and letters. Therefore, for an address to be different from another address it must be different because of one or more of the following reasons:

1. Numbers(s) different

2. Number(s) omitted

3. Numbers(s) added

4. Letters(s) different

5. Letter(s) omitted

6. Letter(s) added

EXAMPLES:

1. <u>Number(s) different:</u>
2617 West Belmont Drive   2671 West Belmont Drive

The "17" in the left address is transposed to "71" in the right address.

2. <u>Number(s) omitted:</u>
2617 West Belmont Drive   261 West Belmont Drive

The "7" in the left address has been omitted in the right address.

3. <u>Number(s) added:</u>
2617 West Belmont Drive   26171 West Belmont Drive

An additional digit "1" has been added to the right column address.

4. <u>Letter(s) different:</u>
2617 West Belmont Drive   2617 West Bedmont Drive

The "l" in Belmont is changed to "d" in Bedmont.

5. <u>Letter(s) omitted:</u>
2617 West Belmont Drive   2617 West Bemont Drive

The "l" in Belmont is omitted in Bemont.

6. <u>Letter(s) added:</u>
2617 West Belmont Drive   2617 West Belmont Scenic Drive

The word "Scenic" is added to the right side address.

<u>HINT #1:</u>
In the ADDRESS CHECKING section of the test you probably will be instructed to mark the answer space:

"A" if there are no errors (differences) in the two addresses

"B" if there is an error (difference) in the address only

"C" if there is an error (difference) in the ZIP code only

"D" if there is an error (difference) in both the address and ZIP code

Try to have these simple instructions clear in your mind. It will prevent you from losing points from selecting incorrect answers.

Also, be aware that the instructions can change and you may be asked to mark different letters than the ones listed above.

HINT #2:

To increase speed, try comparing groups of letters or numbers instead of comparing single digits and letters.

For example, comparing 3546 to 3564 is much faster than comparing the 3 in the first address to the 3 in the second address, then the 5 in the first address to the 5 in the second address, then the 4 in the first address to the 6 in the second address.... (get the point?). The greater the number of digits and letters that you can compare well at one glance, the faster your speed will be.

HOWEVER: do NOT compare the two addresses with just one sweep of the eyes. For example:

2478 Roget Ave SW   and   2478 Roget Ave WS

Compare 2478 and 2478 (Same)

Compare Roget Ave and Roget Ave (Same)

Compare SW and WS (Different)

            Or

Compare 2478 and 2478 (Same)

Compare Roget Ave SW and Roget Ave WS   (Different)

Remember that it is NOT crucial which segments you compare as long as they are not too short or too long. Short segments, such as individual letters and digits, will slow you down and prevent you from maximizing your score. Segments which are too long for you to quickly and accurately compare might cause you to make mistakes and lose precious points.

HINT #3:

"Practice makes perfect."

Practice address checking exercises every day from now until the test. You will be amazed at how much you will improve.

HINT #4:

Work quickly and accurately.

You are allowed approximately 10 seconds for each address comparison.

TRY NOT TO LET YOUR MIND WANDER - even for a second.

Do not let unusual or interesting words distract you.

Consider the following:

47 Snow White St.   47 Snow White Ave.

If upon reading the above addresses you entertain visions of Snow White and the Seven Dwarfs or visions of snow white mountains or visions of brilliant teeth, you may lose a valuable second or two - and even worse become distracted from the difference in the two addresses (St. and Ave.).

HINT #5:

Because the score is calculated by taking the number of correct answers and deducting from it 1/3 of the number of incorrect answers, it is **not** wise to guess blindly on this part of the test.

However, you should not focus on an address pair until you are 200 per cent sure you have the correct answer. A second wasted is a second you could be working on the next address.

HINT #6:

When comparing addresses, do not whisper or read out loud. The mind works much faster than vocal muscles. In other words, do NOT sound out the addresses.

HINT #7:

Make sure your mind sees what is actually there and not what it thinks should be there.

Do not read so fast that you skip words. During your school years your mind might have developed shortcuts that you might not be fully aware of.

Address Checking Examples

On the following page there are 15 address checking examples. The answers and explanations are on the page after that.

1. Read the instructions at the top of the page, then place a sheet of paper on the page where the answers are.

2. Do the 15 examples. The aim is to get familiar with this type of question. At this point do not be concerned about the speed of answering the questions. That will come with practice.

3. Check your answers. How did you do? Chances are that no matter how well you did, you will improve with practice.

4. Following this exercise there are four more exercises with answer explanations.

After you complete these additional four exercises, you will be ready for the five exercises with 30 questions, and later on for the seven practice tests, each with 60 address checking questions.

Whenever there is a time limit specified for that section, stop working at the end of that time limit. This will give you a sense of how quickly you are answering the questions.

(Please note: All the addresses and ZIP codes are fictitious and for practice only.)

The "A", "B", "C", "D" answer circles are to the right of each question.

To indicate your answer, quickly darken the appropriate circle.

The actual test will be on a computer and you will not need a pencil to indicate your answer. You will simply click on the correct answer.

When you are ready, turn the page. Cover the 15 answers on the page on the right and then answer the 15 address checking questions on the left page.

(These examples are intended to help you become used to this type of question and are therefore not timed.)

Address Checking Example 1: Below is a list of 15 pairs of addresses. Compare each pair of addresses for errors and mark the answer sheet to indicate errors found as follows:

A. No errors

B. Errors in address only

C. Errors in Zip Code only

D. Errors in both address and Zip Code

	Correct List of Addresses		Address List to be Checked		Answer Grid
	Address	**ZIP**	**Address**	**ZIP**	
1	283 Fairbiew Cir. Classon, PA	09112	283 Fairbiew Cir. Classon, PA	09121	Ⓐ Ⓑ Ⓒ Ⓓ
2	4869 Tarp Terrace Albany, NY	28403-4235	4869 Tarp Terrace Albany, NY	28403-4235	Ⓐ Ⓑ Ⓒ Ⓓ
3	1792 Wilford Ave. Vernell, VA	66093-0010	1729 Wilford Ave. Vernell, VA	66093-0010	Ⓐ Ⓑ Ⓒ Ⓓ
4	P.O. Box 2702 Justino, FL	10004-7129	P.O. Box 2720 Justino, FL	10004-7192	Ⓐ Ⓑ Ⓒ Ⓓ
5	5700 Wilford Ln. Foly, FL	88913	5700 Wilfurd Ln. Foly, FL	89813	Ⓐ Ⓑ Ⓒ Ⓓ
6	882 Milton Ave. Meteor, MN	24112-3443	882 Milfon Ave. Meteor, MN	24121-3443	Ⓐ Ⓑ Ⓒ Ⓓ
7	713 James Ct. Parton, IL	40201	731 James Ct. Parton, IL	40501	Ⓐ Ⓑ Ⓒ Ⓓ
8	2862 West 6 Street Freely, NJ	36202-8941	2862 East 6 Street Freely, NJ	36202-8941	Ⓐ Ⓑ Ⓒ Ⓓ
9	3724 Talbot Way Wantak, TX	27529	3724 Talbot Way Wantak, TX	27529	Ⓐ Ⓑ Ⓒ Ⓓ
10	6944 Arizona Lane Bekker, AR	72696	6944 Arizona Lane Bekker, AR	76296	Ⓐ Ⓑ Ⓒ Ⓓ
11	9431 Lionel St. Hurmon, OR	79041-1349	9431 Lionel St. Harmon, OR	79041-1349	Ⓐ Ⓑ Ⓒ Ⓓ
12	10 Arlington Rd. Tanning, KS	74899-6749	10 Arlington Rd. Tanning, KS	74899-6449	Ⓐ Ⓑ Ⓒ Ⓓ
13	4820 Zebra Road Alouda, MI	76262-2556	4820 Zedra Road Alouda, MI	76262-2256	Ⓐ Ⓑ Ⓒ Ⓓ
14	1724 Trapper St. Gaynor, AK	78240	1724 Trapper St. Gaynor, AK	78240	Ⓐ Ⓑ Ⓒ Ⓓ
15	6735 Vestor Pkwy. Niles, RI	29220-3189	6735 Westor Pkwy. Niles, RI	29220-3189	Ⓐ Ⓑ Ⓒ Ⓓ

Address Checking Example 1

	Answers
1	**C.** Errors in Zip Code only: 09112 and 09121
2	**A.** No errors
3	**B.** Errors in address only: 1792 and 1729
4	**D.** Errors in both address and Zip Code: 2702 and 2720, 10004-7129 and 10004-7192
5	**D.** Errors in both address and Zip Code: Wilford and Wilfurd, 88913 and 89813
6	**D.** Errors in both address and Zip Code: Milton and Milfon, 24112-3443 and 24121-3443
7	**D.** Errors in both address and Zip Code: 713 and 731, 40201 and 40501
8	**B.** Errors in address only: West and East
9	**A.** No errors
10	**C.** Errors in Zip Code only: 72696 and 76296
11	**B.** Errors in address only: Hurmon and Harmon
12	**C.** Errors in Zip Code only: 74899-6749 and 74899-6449
13	**D.** Errors in both address and Zip Code: Zebra and Zedra, 76262-2556 and 76262-2256
14	**A.** No errors
15	**B.** Errors in address only: Vestor and Westor

Address Checking Example 2: Below is a list of 15 pairs of addresses. Compare each pair of addresses for errors and mark the answer sheet to indicate errors found as follows:

A. No Errors   **B.** Address Only   **C.** Zip Code Only   **D.** Both Address and ZIP Code

Correct List of Addresses   Address List to be Checked

	Address	ZIP	Address	ZIP	Answer Grid
1	1832 Easy Road Tropper, MA	44562	1832 Easy Road Tropper, MA	44562	Ⓐ Ⓑ Ⓒ Ⓓ
2	8842 Fern Pkwy. Corville, OH	13101-6261	8842 Furn Pkwy. Corville, OH	13701-6261	Ⓐ Ⓑ Ⓒ Ⓓ
3	6324 Custard Rd. Sackett, AR	84755	6324 Custurd Rd. Sackett, AR	84755	Ⓐ Ⓑ Ⓒ Ⓓ
4	3517 York St. Nantucket, CA	59321	3577 York St. Nantucket, CA	59821	Ⓐ Ⓑ Ⓒ Ⓓ
5	1618 Foley Street Deloitte, MO	22789-2211	1618 Foley Street Deloitte, MO	22789-2211	Ⓐ Ⓑ Ⓒ Ⓓ
6	5163 Clark Way Balliard, WA	35405	5163 Clark Way Balliard, WA	35505	Ⓐ Ⓑ Ⓒ Ⓓ
7	P.O. Box 971 Kensington, ME	43338-0002	P.O. Box 971 Kensington, ME	43338-0002	Ⓐ Ⓑ Ⓒ Ⓓ
8	48 Harrison Ln. Poplar, SC	26805-2783	48 Harison Ln. Poplar, SC	26805-2783	Ⓐ Ⓑ Ⓒ Ⓓ
9	793 Union Street Bedington, MS	04415-2174	793 Onion Street Bedington, MS	04415-2774	Ⓐ Ⓑ Ⓒ Ⓓ
10	262 Warington Ln. Waters, MI	55748	262 Warington Ln. Waters, MI	55748	Ⓐ Ⓑ Ⓒ Ⓓ
11	184 Vander Ct. Tourmont, AK	58346	184 Vander Ct. Tourmont, AK	58349	Ⓐ Ⓑ Ⓒ Ⓓ
12	1816 Isle Terrace Walket, CT	10007-3614	1816 Isle Terrace Walket, CT	10007-3914	Ⓐ Ⓑ Ⓒ Ⓓ
13	3984 Dyker St. Riccard, MD	03764	3984 Diker St. Riccard, MD	03764	Ⓐ Ⓑ Ⓒ Ⓓ
14	672 Broad Cir. Bluepath, MS	03017-4644	672 Broad St. Bluepath, MS	03017-4644	Ⓐ Ⓑ Ⓒ Ⓓ
15	672 Broad Cir. Cascade, GA	05392	672 Brad Cir. Cascade, GA	05392	Ⓐ Ⓑ Ⓒ Ⓓ

Address Checking Example 2

	Answers
1	**A.** No Errors
2	**D.** Both Address and ZIP Code: Fern and Furn, 13101-6261 and 13701-6261
3	**B.** Address Only: Custard and Custurd
4	**D.** Both Address and ZIP Code: 3517 and 3577, 59321 and 59821
5	**A.** No Errors
6	**C.** Zip Code Only: 35405 and 35505
7	**A.** No Errors
8	**B.** Address Only: Harrison and Harison
9	**D.** Both Address and ZIP Code: Union and Onion, 04415-2174 and 04415-2774
10	**A.** No Errors
11	**C.** Zip Code Only: 58346 and 58349
12	**C.** Zip Code Only: 10007-3614 and 10007-3914
13	**B.** Dyker and Diker
14	**B.** Address only. Cir. and St.
15	**B.** Address Only: Broad and Brad

Address Checking Example 3: Below is a list of 15 pairs of addresses. Compare each pair of addresses for errors and mark the answer sheet to indicate errors found as follows:

A. No Errors   **B.** Address Only   **C.** Zip Code Only   **D.** Both Address and ZIP Code

<table>
<tr><th colspan="2">Correct List of Addresses</th><th colspan="2">Address List to be Checked</th><th></th></tr>
<tr><th></th><th>Address</th><th>ZIP</th><th>Address</th><th>ZIP</th><th>Answer Grid</th></tr>
<tr><td>1</td><td>6713 Clifford Road Boyd, NJ</td><td>33221-2434</td><td>6713 Clifford Road Boyd, NJ</td><td>33221-2434</td><td>Ⓐ Ⓑ Ⓒ Ⓓ</td></tr>
<tr><td>2</td><td>9234 Kings Ave. Bramen, PA</td><td>04201</td><td>9234 Kings Ave. Bramen, PA</td><td>04210</td><td>Ⓐ Ⓑ Ⓒ Ⓓ</td></tr>
<tr><td>3</td><td>4801 Tiger St. Tracker, GA</td><td>63022-9814</td><td>4801 Tigger St. Tracker, GA</td><td>63022-9814</td><td>Ⓐ Ⓑ Ⓒ Ⓓ</td></tr>
<tr><td>4</td><td>8713 Holiday Rd Aden, NY</td><td>72925</td><td>8713 Holliday Rd Aden, NY</td><td>79225</td><td>Ⓐ Ⓑ Ⓒ Ⓓ</td></tr>
<tr><td>5</td><td>24 Headley Cir. Bellor, WA</td><td>26594</td><td>24 Hadley Cir. Bellor, WA</td><td>26594</td><td>Ⓐ Ⓑ Ⓒ Ⓓ</td></tr>
<tr><td>6</td><td>3316 Divine Street Smallville, RI</td><td>65041-3194</td><td>3316 Divine Street Smallville, RI</td><td>65041-3194</td><td>Ⓐ Ⓑ Ⓒ Ⓓ</td></tr>
<tr><td>7</td><td>5751 Crator Way Wooster, MS</td><td>47989-7694</td><td>5751 Crator Way Wooster, MS</td><td>47989-7694</td><td>Ⓐ Ⓑ Ⓒ Ⓓ</td></tr>
<tr><td>8</td><td>P.O. Box 7650 Arcadia, MO</td><td>66161-5265</td><td>P.O. Box 7650 Arcadia, MO</td><td>66161-5565</td><td>Ⓐ Ⓑ Ⓒ Ⓓ</td></tr>
<tr><td>9</td><td>442 Remote Rd. Stenton, MO</td><td>86139</td><td>424 Remote Rd. Stenton, MO</td><td>86139</td><td>Ⓐ Ⓑ Ⓒ Ⓓ</td></tr>
<tr><td>10</td><td>8216 Quaker St. Surry, OH</td><td>18120-1398</td><td>8216 Quakker St. Surry, OH</td><td>18720-1398</td><td>Ⓐ Ⓑ Ⓒ Ⓓ</td></tr>
<tr><td>11</td><td>3371 Pearl Ter Canton, MN</td><td>45561</td><td>3371 Pearl Ter Canton, MN</td><td>45561</td><td>Ⓐ Ⓑ Ⓒ Ⓓ</td></tr>
<tr><td>12</td><td>7342 Contour Ln. Springfield, MI</td><td>12202-1619</td><td>7342 Contour Ln. Springfield, MI</td><td>12202-1919</td><td>Ⓐ Ⓑ Ⓒ Ⓓ</td></tr>
<tr><td>13</td><td>6937 Dairy Pkwy. Singer, RI</td><td>47654</td><td>6937 Dary Pkwy. Singer, RI</td><td>47624</td><td>Ⓐ Ⓑ Ⓒ Ⓓ</td></tr>
<tr><td>14</td><td>2872 Dean Ct. Brookville, CT</td><td>58235</td><td>2872 Dean Cir. Brookville, CT</td><td>58235</td><td>Ⓐ Ⓑ Ⓒ Ⓓ</td></tr>
<tr><td>15</td><td>8132 Florida Ln. Eastville, FL</td><td>21789-4524</td><td>8132 Florida Ln. Eastville, FL</td><td>21189-4524</td><td>Ⓐ Ⓑ Ⓒ Ⓓ</td></tr>
</table>

Address Checking Example 3

	Answers
1	**A.** No Errors
2	**C.** Zip Code Only: 04201 and 04210
3	**B.** Address Only: Tiger and Tigger
4	**D.** Both Address and ZIP Code: Holiday and Holliday, 72925 and 79225
5	**B.** Address Only: Headley and Hadley
6	**A.** No Errors
7	**A.** No Errors
8	**C.** Zip Code Only: 66161-5265 and 66161-5565
9	**B.** Address Only: 442 and 424
10	**D.** Both Address and ZIP Code: Quaker and Quakker, 18120-1398 and 18720-1398
11	**A.** No Errors
12	**C.** Zip Code Only: 12202-1619 and 12202-1919
13	**D.** Both Address and ZIP Code: Dairy and Dary, 47654 and 47624
14	**B.** Address Only: Ct. and Cir.
15	**C.** Zip Code Only: 21789-4524 and 21189-4524

Address Checking Exercise 1: (Time limit 6 min.) Below is a list of 30 pairs of addresses. Compare each pair of addresses for errors and mark the answer sheet as follows:

A. No Errors   **B.** Address Only   **C.** Zip Code Only   **D.** Both Address and ZIP Code

	Correct List of Addresses		Address List to be Checked		
	Address	**ZIP**	**Address**	**ZIP**	**Answer Grid**
1	3283 Summer Ln. Trapper, FL	27210-3186	3283 Sumner Ln. Trapper, FL	27210-3186	A B C D
2	6711 Hector Road Willis, CT	74516	6711 Hektor Road Willis, CT	74516	A B C D
3	P.O. Box 9113 Chorale, MD	21101-1691	P.O. Box 9113 Chorale, MD	21101-1691	A B C D
4	241 Harrison Ave. Savin, MS	69146	241 Harrison Ave. Savin, MS	69746	A B C D
5	241 Lumber Cir. Aruba, CA	76454	241 Lumber St. Aruba, CA	79454	A B C D
6	6377 Contract Ln. Kayton, AK	32678-3642	6377 Contract Ln. Kayton, AK	32678-3645	A B C D
7	672 Bravo Street Greenville, SC	63405	672 Bravo Street Greenview, SC	63402	A B C D
8	7714 Clifford Rd. Irving, VA	45238-0130	7114 Clifford Rd. Irving, VA	45238-0130	A B C D
9	4321 Irving Ave. Sycamore, MI	03565-6192	4327 Irving Ave. Sycamore, MI	03565-6195	A B C D
10	5226 Ray Way Pounder, RI	16057-7121	5226 Ray Way Pounder, RI	16057-7121	A B C D
11	7618 Waret St. Enderton, KS	36371	7618 Waret St. Enderton, KS	36871	A B C D
12	9641 Gator St. Endville, MO	45163	9641 Gator St. Endville, MO	45763	A B C D
13	8112 Quarter Ave. Bath Beach, CA	06432	8112 Quarter Ave. Bath Beach, CA	06432	A B C D
14	5734 People Lane Benson, CA	06432	5734 People Lane Benton, CA	06482	A B C D
15	672 Lifton Ct. Menington, CT	09513	672 Lifton Ct. Meninton, CT	09513	A B C D

Address Checking Exercise 1 (cont'd): Continue to compare each pair of addresses for errors and mark the answer sheet as follows:

A. No Errors   **B.** Address Only   **C.** Zip Code Only   **D.** Both Address and ZIP Code

	Correct List of Addresses		Address List to be Checked		
	Address	**ZIP**	**Address**	**ZIP**	**Answer Grid**
16	3397 Eastern Rd. Nippon, CA	02182-4634	3379 Eastern Rd.	02182-4634	A B C D
17	5519 Silver Ln. Strummer, AK	07317	5519 Silver Ln. Strumner, AK	07317	A B C D
18	615 Jasper Ave. Shephard, NY	26204-1518	615 Jasper Ave. Shepard, NY	26204-7518	A B C D
19	8114 South Way East Port, MD	33291-0379	8114 South Way East Port, MD	33291-0376	A B C D
20	7237 Kramer St. Salem, MO	39213-7718	7237 Kramer St. Salem, MO	39213-7718	A B C D
21	933 Media Pkwy. Arlo, WA	21726	933 Media Pkwy. Arlo, WA	27726	A B C D
22	2482 Candle St. Seneca, NJ	05113-2168	2482 Candle St. Seneka, NJ	05113-2163	A B C D
23	7119 Luke Ct. Waverly, MI	04772	7119 Luke Ct. Waverly, MI	04772	A B C D
24	2124 Spring Cir. Davenville, CT	38151-7220	2124 Spring Cir. Davenville, CT	38151-7250	A B C D
25	3436 West Ave. Bunsky, KS	34824-1080	3436 West Ave. Bundy, KS	34824-1080	A B C D
26	5813 Clover St. Mastic, OH	45132-6762	5818 Clover St. Mastic, OH	45132-6162	A B C D
27	92 Main Road Lepper, RI	32747	92 Main Road Lemper, RI	35747	A B C D
28	P.O. Box 3731 Brassford, ME	71222-4244	P.O. Box 3731 Brassford, ME	71222-4244	A B C D
29	68 Canary St. Tucker, CA	06322	63 Canary St. Tucker, CA	06322	A B C D
30	746 Corner Lane Ford, FL	83024-8941	746 Corner Lane Fords, FL	83024-8941	A B C D

Address Checking Exercise 2: (Time limit 6 min.) Below is a list of 30 pairs of addresses. Compare each pair of addresses for errors and mark the answer sheet as follows:

A. No Errors   **B.** Address Only   **C.** Zip Code Only   **D.** Both Address and ZIP Code

Correct List of Addresses   **Address List to be Checked**

	Address	ZIP	Address	ZIP	Answer Grid
1	5512 Norway Ct. Appler, MS	37286	5512 Norway Ct. Appler, MS	37289	Ⓐ Ⓑ Ⓒ Ⓓ
2	3837 Norman Ave. Bay View, CT	73946	3837 Normen Ave. Bay View, CT	73946	Ⓐ Ⓑ Ⓒ Ⓓ
3	1924 Bush St. Miller, IL	67412-5250	1924 Bush St. Miner, IL	67472-5250	Ⓐ Ⓑ Ⓒ Ⓓ
4	72 Constitution Ln. Tarkadered, OR	70282-5263	72 Constitution Ln. Tarkadered, OR	70282-5263	Ⓐ Ⓑ Ⓒ Ⓓ
5	P.O. Box 813 Olsen, OR	48877-7594	P.O. Box 8133 Olsen, OR	48877-7594	Ⓐ Ⓑ Ⓒ Ⓓ
6	7337 Maloney Rd. Carroway, VA	37221-4285	7337 Maloney Rd. Caroway, VA	37251-4285	Ⓐ Ⓑ Ⓒ Ⓓ
7	4684 Optimum St. Corvette, TX	85347	4684 Optimum St. Corvelle, TX	85357	Ⓐ Ⓑ Ⓒ Ⓓ
8	3731 Military Way North King, NY	85417	3731 Military Way North King, NY	85471	Ⓐ Ⓑ Ⓒ Ⓓ
9	6118 Evelyn Street South Bay, PA	32110-2792	6118 Evlyn Street South Bay, PA	32110-2792	Ⓐ Ⓑ Ⓒ Ⓓ
10	8156 Mexico Ave. Parish, FL	69461	8156 Mexico Ave. Parish, FL	69491	Ⓐ Ⓑ Ⓒ Ⓓ
11	6713 Fern Terrace Oakville, MN	76543	6713 Fern Terrace Oakville, MN	76548	Ⓐ Ⓑ Ⓒ Ⓓ
12	7548 Proper St. Homer, AR	33766-1643	7548 Prosper St. Homer, AR	33766-1643	Ⓐ Ⓑ Ⓒ Ⓓ
13	172 Beach Cir. Herkimer, NJ	73406	172 Beach Cir. Herkimur, NJ	73409	Ⓐ Ⓑ Ⓒ Ⓓ
14	4713 Miranda Rd Quiet Bay, MA	55237-2104	4713 Miranda Rd Quiet Bay, MA	55237-2104	Ⓐ Ⓑ Ⓒ Ⓓ
15	3273 Busy Pkwy. Lakeview, SC	17175-7079	3273 Buzy Pkwy. Lakeview, SC	17175-7079	Ⓐ Ⓑ Ⓒ Ⓓ

Address Checking Exercise 2 (cont'd): Continue to compare each pair of addresses for errors and mark the answer sheet as follows:

A. No Errors   **B.** Address Only   **C.** Zip Code Only   **D.** Both Address and ZIP Code

	Correct List of Addresses		Address List to be Checked		
	Address	**ZIP**	**Address**	**ZIP**	**Answer Grid**
16	6347 Classic Rd. S. Monica, CA	14433-7293	6347 Classic Rd. S. Monica, CA	14438-7293	A B C D
17	1876 Gate Ln. Ryder, NY	47462	1876 Gate Ln. Ryder, NY	47462	A B C D
18	1072 Ellenby St. Collier, PA	55274	1072 Ellendy St. Collier, PA	55274	A B C D
19	681 Dickens St. Harvey, CA	10004-0468	681 Dikkens St. Harvey, CA	10004-0498	A B C D
20	P.O.Box 2184 Pinnacle, VA	08543	P.O.Box 2184 Pinnacle, VA	08243	A B C D
21	2816 Wayly Rd. Montview, MN	87531	2816 Wayly Rd. Montview, MN	87581	A B C D
22	3492 Monaor Ct. Steiner, SC	21083-6735	3492 Monor Ct. Steiner, SC	21083-6735	A B C D
23	746 Vetran St. South End, NY	37103-2692	746 Vetran St. South End, NJ	37103-2629	A B C D
24	593 Forest Ter. Dinkens, IL	43390-1396	593 Forest Ter. Dinkens, IL	43390-1396	A B C D
25	4252 Mexo Ave. Fuller, MA	38414-6617	4225 Mexo Ave. Fuller, MA	38414-6617	A B C D
26	7189 Darby St. Molly, AR	32625	7189 Darcy St. Molly, AR	32622	A B C D
27	632 Boxer Cir. Rangoon, NJ	15321-6182	632 Boxers Cir. Rangoon, NJ	15321-6182	A B C D
28	9726 Brad Rd. Martin, TX	05681	9726 Brad Rd. Martin, TX	05981	A B C D
29	3582 Zebra Lane Pacific, FL	47252-8331	3582 Zebra Lane Pacific, FL	47255-8331	A B C D
30	3746 Candle St. Brooklyn, NY	11285	3746 Candle St. Brooklyn, NY	11285	A B C D

Address Checking Exercise 3: (Time limit 6 min.) Below is a list of 30 pairs of addresses. Compare each pair of addresses for errors and mark the answer sheet as follows:

A. No Errors   **B.** Address Only   **C.** Zip Code Only   **D.** Both Address and ZIP Code

	Correct List of Addresses		Address List to be Checked		
	Address	**ZIP**	**Address**	**ZIP**	**Answer Grid**
1	5062 Flower St. Culty, MO	35383-2181	5062 Flower St. Culty, MO	35383-2187	Ⓐ Ⓑ Ⓒ Ⓓ
2	183 Eastern Pkwy. Puller, ME	46133-6863	183 Eastern Pkwy. Pulter, ME	46733-6863	Ⓐ Ⓑ Ⓒ Ⓓ
3	7002 Marlow Ln. Commons, MD	43849	7002 Marlow Ln. Commons, MD	43849	Ⓐ Ⓑ Ⓒ Ⓓ
4	1791 Ferndale Cir. Century, MS	82113-5145	1791 Ferndale Cir. Century, MS	85113-5145	Ⓐ Ⓑ Ⓒ Ⓓ
5	4447 Welford St. Exeter, OH	07433	4447 Wellford St. Exeter, OH	07433	Ⓐ Ⓑ Ⓒ Ⓓ
6	3912 Red Road Long Falls, KS	92113-7852	3912 Red Road Lang Falls, KS	92173-7852	Ⓐ Ⓑ Ⓒ Ⓓ
7	P.O. Box 5937 Hamlet, WA	48397	P.O. Box 5937 Hamlet, WA	48397	Ⓐ Ⓑ Ⓒ Ⓓ
8	98 Hems Rd. Booker, CT	84057	98 Hems Rd. Bocker, CT	84057	Ⓐ Ⓑ Ⓒ Ⓓ
9	6394 Finn Pkwy. Foulder, MI	78124-5358	6894 Finn Pkwy. Foulder, MI	78124-5358	Ⓐ Ⓑ Ⓒ Ⓓ
10	9283 Pumpkin St. Bemington, MI	49776-7605	9283 Pumpkin St. Bemington, MI	49776-7905	Ⓐ Ⓑ Ⓒ Ⓓ
11	2426 Flavos St. Puller, AK	81384-5367	2426 Flavor St. Puller, AK	81384-5367	Ⓐ Ⓑ Ⓒ Ⓓ
12	3912 Hudson Ave. Atlantic, RI	96458	3912 Hadson Ave. Atlantic, RI	96458	Ⓐ Ⓑ Ⓒ Ⓓ
13	5782 Tibet Lane Mirage, AR	38321-5394	5782 Tibet Lane Mirage, AR	38321-5894	Ⓐ Ⓑ Ⓒ Ⓓ
14	661 Martin Ct. Bayshore, PA	94318	661 Martin Ct. Bayshore, PA	94318	Ⓐ Ⓑ Ⓒ Ⓓ
15	7664 Govern Lane West Lake, CA	43221-2894	7694 Govern Lane West Lake, CA	43221-5894	Ⓐ Ⓑ Ⓒ Ⓓ

Address Checking Exercise 3 (cont'd): Continue to compare each pair of addresses for errors and mark the answer sheet as follows:

A. No Errors   **B.** Address Only   **C.** Zip Code Only   **D.** Both Address and ZIP Code

	Correct List of Addresses		Address List to be Checked		
	Address	**ZIP**	**Address**	**ZIP**	**Answer Grid**
16	940 Albany St. Albany, CA	87644	640 Albany St. Albany, CA	37644	Ⓐ Ⓑ Ⓒ Ⓓ
17	2872 Brend St. King City, SC	70562	2872 Brend St. King City, SC	70562	Ⓐ Ⓑ Ⓒ Ⓓ
18	2105 Nap Ave. Huron, KS	44867-2741	2105 Nap Ave. Huron, KS	44867-2741	Ⓐ Ⓑ Ⓒ Ⓓ
19	158 Lorraine Ct. Perris, MO	84315	158 Lorraine Ct. Perris, MO	84375	Ⓐ Ⓑ Ⓒ Ⓓ
20	7328 Monk St. Huron, MD	45326-3214	7828 Monk St. Huron, MD	45325-3214	Ⓐ Ⓑ Ⓒ Ⓓ
21	7625 Back Ter. Hemet, OH	28271-8197	7625 Back Ter. Hemet, OH	28271-8197	Ⓐ Ⓑ Ⓒ Ⓓ
22	1193 Avelon St. Pomona, MS	43541-2937	1193 Avellon St. Pomona, MS	43541-2931	Ⓐ Ⓑ Ⓒ Ⓓ
23	4182 Navy Way Gustine, NY	74624	4182 Navy Way Gustine, NY	74924	Ⓐ Ⓑ Ⓒ Ⓓ
24	2446 Spre Lane Rialto, TX	52745	2446 Sore Lake Rialto, TX	52742	Ⓐ Ⓑ Ⓒ Ⓓ
25	776 Statter Cir. Bishop, MI	01004-4680	776 Statler Cir. Bishop, MI	01004-4680	Ⓐ Ⓑ Ⓒ Ⓓ
26	899 Reserve Ln. Marina, WA	85430	896 Reserve Ln. Marina, WA	85430	Ⓐ Ⓑ Ⓒ Ⓓ
27	P.O. Box 1821 Brea, PA	78531	P.O. Box 1851 Brea, PA	78231	Ⓐ Ⓑ Ⓒ Ⓓ
28	8246 Step Rd. Tracy, ME	12083-7355	8246 Step Rd. Tracy, ME	12083-7355	Ⓐ Ⓑ Ⓒ Ⓓ
29	5326 India Road Malibu, RI	74281	5326 India Road Malibu, RI	74581	Ⓐ Ⓑ Ⓒ Ⓓ
30	3424 District St. Montclair, NJ	31730-6291	3454 District St. Montclair, NJ	31730-6291	Ⓐ Ⓑ Ⓒ Ⓓ

Address Checking Exercise #1 Answers

1	B	6	C	11	C	16	B	21	C	26	D
2	B	7	D	12	C	17	B	22	D	27	D
3	A	8	B	13	A	18	D	23	A	28	A
4	C	9	D	14	D	19	C	24	D	29	B
5	D	10	A	15	B	20	A	25	B	30	B

Address Checking Exercise #2 Answers

1	C	6	D	11	C	16	C	21	C	26	D
2	B	7	D	12	B	17	A	22	B	27	B
3	D	8	C	13	D	18	B	23	D	28	C
4	A	9	B	14	A	19	D	24	A	29	C
5	B	10	C	15	B	20	C	25	B	30	A

Address Checking Exercise #3 Answers

1	C	6	D	11	B	16	D	21	A	26	B
2	D	7	A	12	B	17	A	22	D	27	D
3	A	8	B	13	C	18	A	23	C	28	A
4	C	9	B	14	A	19	C	24	D	29	C
5	B	10	C	15	D	20	D	25	B	30	B

"I know the price of success: dedication, hard work and an unremitting devotion to the things you want to see happen."

-Frank Lloyd Wright

FORMS COMPLETION

2

Postal employees come in contact with postal forms every day. Sometimes postal employees have to complete forms. Sometimes they must review them for accuracy.

To work efficiently and with minimal errors, a postal employee must understand forms and be comfortable with their use.

Part	Time Allowed	Number of Ques.	Description of Question
2. Forms Completion	**15 minutes**	**30**	**Correctly complete forms.**

The forms completion section of the postal test presents you with sample forms which you must use to answer 30 questions within the allotted 15 minutes.

(The forms used in this book are not USPS forms. If you wish to review official USPS forms, please visit: www.USPS.com)

IMPORTANT!	On this forms completion part of the test there is **NO** penalty for guessing. You **will** receive credit if you guess correctly. You will **NOT** be penalized if you guess incorrectly. Therefore, you should answer all 30 questions, even if you have to guess on some of them.

Hint #1:

Look at the form carefully.

1. Title of form (What is the purpose of the form?)
2. Titles of sections (Who is responsible for filling out each section?)
3. What information is asked for in each section?

    (Address, description of contents of package, postage, other fees, etc.)

Hint #2:

Answer **ALL** the questions. If you don't know the answer, **GUESS.**

In this section there is NO penalty for guessing wrong.

Hint #3:

Keep in mind that this section is timed (30 questions in 15 minutes). Try to work as quickly and accurately as you can.

Do **NOT** linger on a question until you are 200% certain that you answered correctly.

Hint #4:

Try to look at as many official USPS forms as you can. USPS forms may be found online at www.USPS.com.

The more familiar and comfortable you become with these forms, the greater the likelihood that you will attain a high score.

———————

The following pages contain 3 practice forms.

These forms, like all other forms in this book, are for practice and are not USPS forms.

Examine each form. Take as long as you wish. These 3 examples are not timed.

The purpose of these forms and questions relating to them is to provide you with brief exercises to help you develop an approach to tackling this type of question. Later, in the three practice tests, you will have timed practice.

Good luck!

FORMS COMPLETION EXAMPLE #1

Study the following form, then answer the following 10 questions about the form.

(This practice example is not timed.)

1. RECEIPT FOR INSURED MAIL		
15.	2. Postage	6. ☐ Fragile 7. ☐ Perishable
		8. ☐ Liquid 9. ☐ Hazardous
	3. Insurance Fee	10.
		11. Stamp Postmark Here
	4. Handling Fee	
	5. Total (Postage plus Fees) $_____	
12. Addressee (Sent to):		
13. Street, Apt. Number; or PO Box Number		
14. City, State and ZIP		

	Question	Answer Grid
1	The name of the person or company to whom the article is sent to should be entered in box : A. 13　　　B. 12　　　C. 14　　　D. 10	Ⓐ Ⓑ Ⓒ Ⓓ
2	The postmark should be properly stamped in area: A. 15　　　B. 2　　　C. 5　　　D. 11	Ⓐ Ⓑ Ⓒ Ⓓ
3	Where on this form should the ZIP number of the addressee be entered? A. 11　　　B. 12　　　C. 13　　　D. 14	Ⓐ Ⓑ Ⓒ Ⓓ

4	Which of the following is a correct entry for box 4? A. 6/12/10 B. NYC C. $6.50 D. Fragile	Ⓐ Ⓑ Ⓒ Ⓓ
5	The contents of the article include fresh New York State apples. Because of this, which of the following boxes should be checked? A. 9 B. 7 C. 14 D. 10	Ⓐ Ⓑ Ⓒ Ⓓ
6	A $25.00 insurance fee was paid. In which box should this be indicated? A. 2 B. 12 C. 3 D. 10	Ⓐ Ⓑ Ⓒ Ⓓ
7	Total paid for postage was $10.00. The total paid for other fees was $6.00 ($3.00 insurance fee plus $3.00 handling fee). The amount that should be entered in box 5 is: A. $10.00 B. $6.00 C. $16.00 D. $13.00	Ⓐ Ⓑ Ⓒ Ⓓ
8	In which box would you indicate that the item is dangerous and should be handled carefully? A. 6 B. 7 C. 8 D. 9	Ⓐ Ⓑ Ⓒ Ⓓ
9	Which of the following is a correct entry in box 13? A. Fragile B. $3.95 C. 14 Hale St. D. New York City	Ⓐ Ⓑ Ⓒ Ⓓ
10	A money amount is a correct entry for each of the following boxes, except: A. 11 B. 4 C. 3 D. 2	Ⓐ Ⓑ Ⓒ Ⓓ

(Answers are on page 38.)

FORMS COMPLETION EXAMPLE #2

Study the following form, then answer the following 9 questions about the form.

(This practice example is not timed.)

1. RETURN RECEIPT FOR DOMESTIC MAIL		
THIS SECTION IS TO BE COMPLETED BY THE SENDER	**THIS SECTION IS TO BE COMPLETED UPON DELIVERY OF THE ITEM**	
2. ▶Sender must complete items 5, 6, (and 12, 13, 14, 15, 16, 17, 18, if applicable.) 3. ▶Sender must print sender's name and address on the reverse side of this card so that card can be returned to sender. 4. ▶Peel off glue protector strips on opposite side and attach to the back of the mail, or on the front if there is enough space.	7. Signature □ Addressee ▶ □ Agent	
	8. Received by (PRINT)	9. Delivery Date
	10. Is delivery address same or different from item 5? □ Same □ Different (If different, write delivery address below:	
5. Article addressed to:	Type of mail service:	
	12. □ Registered	15. □ C.O.D.
	13. □ Insured	16. □ Express
	14. □ Certified	17. □ Merchandise Return receipt
	18. Restricted delivery (Additional fee) $_____ □ Yes	
6. Article number (from service label)		

	Question	Answer Grid
1	Which of the following items is never completed by the sender? A. 15 B. 18 C. 14 D. 7	Ⓐ Ⓑ Ⓒ Ⓓ
2	The address of the addressee is entered in box: A. 6 B. 12 C. 5 D. 9	Ⓐ Ⓑ Ⓒ Ⓓ

3	Where does one get the "article number"? A. bulletin board B. newspaper C. service label D. None of the above	Ⓐ Ⓑ Ⓒ Ⓓ
4	Which of the following is a correct entry for box 8? A. 6/12/10 B. John Kern C. $6.50 D. Fragile	Ⓐ Ⓑ Ⓒ Ⓓ
5	If the article is to be mailed by express mail, which box must be checked off? A. 5 B. 16 C. 6 D. 14	Ⓐ Ⓑ Ⓒ Ⓓ
6	If an agent of the addressee receives the mail, the addressee's agent must print h is name in box: A. 7 B. 8 C. 6 D. 10	Ⓐ Ⓑ Ⓒ Ⓓ
7	The darkened section of this form must be completed by: A. sender B. postal employee only C. postal supervisor D. None of the above	Ⓐ Ⓑ Ⓒ Ⓓ
8	In which box would you indicate that the type of mail service is "Certified"? A. 14 B. 15 C. 18 D. 10	Ⓐ Ⓑ Ⓒ Ⓓ
9	Which of the following is a correct entry in box 9? A. 3:00 p.m. B. 12/10 C. 7/14/10 D. 24:02	Ⓐ Ⓑ Ⓒ Ⓓ

(Answers are on page 38.)

FORMS COMPLETION EXAMPLE #3

Study the following form, then answer the following 7 questions about the form.

(This practice example is not timed.)

RECEIPT FOR REGISTERED MAIL			
:	2.Registered Number	4. Date Stamp	
1.This section is to be completed by the post office.	3. Registration Fee $ _____	5. Charge for Handling	8. Fee for Return Receipt
		6. Postage Amount	9. Fee for Restricted Delivery
		7. Received by	
10. This section is to be completed by the postal customer. Please PRINT with ballpoint pen, or TYPE.	11. TO:		
	12. FROM:		
FORM # 7477 (Copy 1 – Customer) (Copy 2 – Post Office) (See information on reverse side of this form.)			

	Question	Answer Grid
1	The name of the person or company to whom the article is sent to should be entered in box : A. 12　　　　B. 11　　　　C. 10　　　　D. 1	Ⓐ Ⓑ Ⓒ Ⓓ
2	The date should be stamped by the post office in box: A. 1　　　　B. 10　　　　C. 4　　　　D. 11	Ⓐ Ⓑ Ⓒ Ⓓ
3	Where on this form should the ZIP number of the addressee be entered? A. 11　　　　B. 12　　　　C. 2　　　　D. 4	Ⓐ Ⓑ Ⓒ Ⓓ
4	Which of the following is a correct entry for box 3? A. insured　　　B. 12/11/10　　　C. 7.50　　　D. #3	Ⓐ Ⓑ Ⓒ Ⓓ
5	Which of the following boxes should not be completed by the post office? A. 4　　　　B. 8　　　　C. 6　　　　D. 12	Ⓐ Ⓑ Ⓒ Ⓓ
6	A $4.75 fee for return receipt was paid. In which box should this be indicated? A. 8　　　　B. 5　　　　C. 9　　　　D. 4	Ⓐ Ⓑ Ⓒ Ⓓ
7	Total paid for postage was $12.00. This amount that should be entered in box: A. 5　　　　B. 6　　　　C. 9　　　　D. 8	Ⓐ Ⓑ Ⓒ Ⓓ

(Answers are on page 38.)

FORMS COMPLETION ANSWERS (EXAMPLES 1 – 3)

#1	#2	#3
1. B	1. D	1. B
2. D	2. C	2. C
3. D	3. C	3. A
4. C	4. B	4. C
5. B	5. B	5. D
6. C	6. B	6. A
7. C	7. D	7. B
8. D	8. A	
9. C	9. C	
10. A		

TRY TO KEEP IN MIND:

Hint #1:

Look at the form carefully.

1. Title of form (What is the purpose of the form?)

2. Titles of sections (Who is responsible for filling out each section?)

3. What information is asked for in each section?

   (Address, description of contents of package, postage, other fees, etc.)

Hint #2:

Answer **ALL** the questions. If you don't know the answer, **GUESS.**

In this section there is NO penalty for guessing wrong.

Hint #3:

Remember that this section is timed (30 questions in 15 minutes). Try to work as quickly and accurately as you can. Do **NOT** linger on a question until you are 200% certain that you answered correctly.

Hint #4:

Try to look at as many official USPS forms as you can. USPS forms may be found online at www.USPS.com.

The more familiar and comfortable you become with these forms, the greater the likelihood that you will attain a high score.

Part	Time Allowed	Number of Ques.	Description of Question
3. Coding	6 minutes	36	**Find correct code for an address.**

In the **CODING** part of the test you will be provided with a table (a Coding Guide).

The format of the Coding Guide will probably be similar to the following coding guide:

Coding Guide

Range of Addresses	Delivery Route
1 - 99 Rochester Avenue 100 - 1000 Bleeker Street 20 - 90 S. 18th Road	A
100 - 300 Rochester Avenue 91 - 200 S. 18th Road	B
5000 - 15000 Jefferson Lane 1 - 100 Rural Route 12 1001 - 5000 Bleeker Street	C
All mail that does not fall in one of address ranges listed above	D

You will be given 36 addresses which fall into one of the listed "Delivery Routes" in the coding guide (Delivery routes A, B, C, D).

Your job will be to determine into which "Delivery Route" each one of the addresses falls into.

For example, 24 Rochester Avenue falls into Delivery Route "A" because 24 Rochester Avenue falls between 1 Rochester Avenue and 99 Rochester Avenue (1 – 99 Rochester Avenue).

6900 Jefferson Lane belongs in Delivery Route "C" because 6900 Jefferson Lane falls between 5000 Jefferson Lane and 15000 Jefferson Lane (5000 – 15000 Jefferson Lane).

The next three addresses belong to Delivery Route "D" because they do not fall within the range of any of the addresses listed in the "Range of Addresses" column.

6000 Bleeker Street,   2856 Adams Street,   301 Rochester Avenue

The following are further examples of correct coding of addresses:

Address	Delivery Route
88 Rural Route 25	D
600 Rochester Avenue	D
25 Rochester Avenue	A
2000 Bleeker Street	C
95 S. 18th Road	B
50 Rural Route 12	C
6000 Jefferson Lane	C
150 Rural Route 12	D
28 Rochester Avenue	A
142 Bleeker Street	A
60 S. 18th Road	A
10000 Jefferson Lane	C

On the test you will be given 36 addresses to code in 6 minutes.

In practicing for this part of the test, your aim should be to work quickly and accurately and finish all 36 addresses in the 6 allotted minutes.

Directions for the following 3 Coding Exercises

For each of the following 3 exercises a "Coding Guide" is provided, followed by 36 addresses.

For each address, determine whether the address belongs to Delivery Route A, B, C or D, and mark your answer sheet accordingly.

You have 6 minutes to complete each of the 3 coding exercises.

(Time limit on each exercise is 6 minutes for 36 questions.)

(Answers are on page 48.)

Good Luck!

Coding Exercise #1:   Coding Guide

Range of Addresses	Delivery Route
1 - 99 Ferndale Avenue 100 - 1000 Hazel Street 20 - 90 S. 12th Road	A
100 - 300 Ferndale Avenue 91 - 200 S. 12th Road	B
5000 - 15000 Lincoln Lane 1 - 100 Rural Route 2 1001 - 5000 Hazel Street	C
All mail that does not fall in one of address ranges listed above	D

	Delivery Address	Delivery Route				Answer Grid
1	6000 Lincoln Lane	A	B	C	D	Ⓐ Ⓑ Ⓒ Ⓓ
2	20 S. 12th Road	A	B	C	D	Ⓐ Ⓑ Ⓒ Ⓓ
3	34 Rural Route 2	A	B	C	D	Ⓐ Ⓑ Ⓒ Ⓓ
4	45 Ferndale Avenue	A	B	C	D	Ⓐ Ⓑ Ⓒ Ⓓ
5	132 S. 12th Road	A	B	C	D	Ⓐ Ⓑ Ⓒ Ⓓ
6	2000 Hazel Street	A	B	C	D	Ⓐ Ⓑ Ⓒ Ⓓ
7	88 S. 12th Road	A	B	C	D	Ⓐ Ⓑ Ⓒ Ⓓ
8	6000 Hazel Street	A	B	C	D	Ⓐ Ⓑ Ⓒ Ⓓ
9	189 Ferndale Avenue	A	B	C	D	Ⓐ Ⓑ Ⓒ Ⓓ
10	55 Rural Route 2	A	B	C	D	Ⓐ Ⓑ Ⓒ Ⓓ
11	25 Ferndale Avenue	A	B	C	D	Ⓐ Ⓑ Ⓒ Ⓓ
12	12500 Lincoln Lane	A	B	C	D	Ⓐ Ⓑ Ⓒ Ⓓ
13	4000 Hazel Street	A	B	C	D	Ⓐ Ⓑ Ⓒ Ⓓ
14	160 Ferndale Avenue	A	B	C	D	Ⓐ Ⓑ Ⓒ Ⓓ

	Delivery Address	Delivery Route				Answer Grid
15	7800 Lincoln Lane	A	B	C	D	(A) (B) (C) (D)
16	5 Ferndale Avenue	A	B	C	D	(A) (B) (C) (D)
17	9000 Hazel Street	A	B	C	D	(A) (B) (C) (D)
18	400 S. 12th Road	A	B	C	D	(A) (B) (C) (D)
19	350 Hazel Street	A	B	C	D	(A) (B) (C) (D)
20	500 Ferndale Avenue	A	B	C	D	(A) (B) (C) (D)
21	50 S. 12th Road	A	B	C	D	(A) (B) (C) (D)
22	290 Ferndale Avenue	A	B	C	D	(A) (B) (C) (D)
23	95 S. 12th Road	A	B	C	D	(A) (B) (C) (D)
24	82 Ferndale Avenue	A	B	C	D	(A) (B) (C) (D)
25	90 Rural Route 2	A	B	C	D	(A) (B) (C) (D)
26	240 S. 12th Road	A	B	C	D	(A) (B) (C) (D)
27	105 Hazel Street	A	B	C	D	(A) (B) (C) (D)
28	147 S. 12th Road	A	B	C	D	(A) (B) (C) (D)
29	5500 Lincoln Lane	A	B	C	D	(A) (B) (C) (D)
30	3300 Hazel Street	A	B	C	D	(A) (B) (C) (D)
31	90 Ferndale Avenue	A	B	C	D	(A) (B) (C) (D)
32	75 S. 12th Road	A	B	C	D	(A) (B) (C) (D)
33	150 Ferndale Avenue	A	B	C	D	(A) (B) (C) (D)
34	16000 Lincoln Lane	A	B	C	D	(A) (B) (C) (D)
35	600 Hazel Street	A	B	C	D	(A) (B) (C) (D)
36	9000 Ferndale Avenue	A	B	C	D	(A) (B) (C) (D)

Coding Exercise #2: Coding Guide

Range of Addresses	Delivery Route
1 - 49 Western Lane 200 - 900 Jennings Street 25 - 75 North Circle	A
50 - 200 Western Lane 76 - 200 North Circle	B
100 - 1200 King Ave. 1 - 100 Furman Route 10 901 - 1000 Jennings Street	C
All mail that doesn't fall in one of the address ranges listed above	D

	Delivery Address	Delivery Route				Answer Grid
1	44 Western Lane	A	B	C	D	Ⓐ Ⓑ Ⓒ Ⓓ
2	1400 King Ave.	A	B	C	D	Ⓐ Ⓑ Ⓒ Ⓓ
3	300 Jennings Street	A	B	C	D	Ⓐ Ⓑ Ⓒ Ⓓ
4	300 Furman Route 10	A	B	C	D	Ⓐ Ⓑ Ⓒ Ⓓ
5	500 King Ave.	A	B	C	D	Ⓐ Ⓑ Ⓒ Ⓓ
6	30 North Circle	A	B	C	D	Ⓐ Ⓑ Ⓒ Ⓓ
7	30 Western Lane	A	B	C	D	Ⓐ Ⓑ Ⓒ Ⓓ
8	1300 North Circle	A	B	C	D	Ⓐ Ⓑ Ⓒ Ⓓ
9	90 Furman Route 10	A	B	C	D	Ⓐ Ⓑ Ⓒ Ⓓ
10	24 Western Lane	A	B	C	D	Ⓐ Ⓑ Ⓒ Ⓓ
11	1100 Jennings Street	A	B	C	D	Ⓐ Ⓑ Ⓒ Ⓓ
12	220 Furman Route 10	A	B	C	D	Ⓐ Ⓑ Ⓒ Ⓓ
13	50 North Circle	A	B	C	D	Ⓐ Ⓑ Ⓒ Ⓓ
14	850 Jennings Street	A	B	C	D	Ⓐ Ⓑ Ⓒ Ⓓ

	Delivery Address	Delivery Route				Answer Grid
15	240 Jennings Street	A	B	C	D	Ⓐ Ⓑ Ⓒ Ⓓ
16	80 North Circle	A	B	C	D	Ⓐ Ⓑ Ⓒ Ⓓ
17	1300 King Ave.	A	B	C	D	Ⓐ Ⓑ Ⓒ Ⓓ
18	55 Western Lane	A	B	C	D	Ⓐ Ⓑ Ⓒ Ⓓ
19	62 Western Lane	A	B	C	D	Ⓐ Ⓑ Ⓒ Ⓓ
20	150 Furman Route 10	A	B	C	D	Ⓐ Ⓑ Ⓒ Ⓓ
21	1220 Jennings Street	A	B	C	D	Ⓐ Ⓑ Ⓒ Ⓓ
22	100 Western Lane	A	B	C	D	Ⓐ Ⓑ Ⓒ Ⓓ
23	600 King Ave.	A	B	C	D	Ⓐ Ⓑ Ⓒ Ⓓ
24	89 North Circle	A	B	C	D	Ⓐ Ⓑ Ⓒ Ⓓ
25	400 Jennings Street	A	B	C	D	Ⓐ Ⓑ Ⓒ Ⓓ
26	85 Furman Route 10	A	B	C	D	Ⓐ Ⓑ Ⓒ Ⓓ
27	60 North Circle	A	B	C	D	Ⓐ Ⓑ Ⓒ Ⓓ
28	950 Jennings Street	A	B	C	D	Ⓐ Ⓑ Ⓒ Ⓓ
29	189 North Circle	A	B	C	D	Ⓐ Ⓑ Ⓒ Ⓓ
30	175 Western Lane	A	B	C	D	Ⓐ Ⓑ Ⓒ Ⓓ
31	1010 Jennings Street	A	B	C	D	Ⓐ Ⓑ Ⓒ Ⓓ
32	92 North Circle	A	B	C	D	Ⓐ Ⓑ Ⓒ Ⓓ
33	700 Jennings Street	A	B	C	D	Ⓐ Ⓑ Ⓒ Ⓓ
34	153 Western Lane	A	B	C	D	Ⓐ Ⓑ Ⓒ Ⓓ
35	140 King Ave.	A	B	C	D	Ⓐ Ⓑ Ⓒ Ⓓ
36	200 Western Lane	A	B	C	D	Ⓐ Ⓑ Ⓒ Ⓓ

Coding Exercise #3:   Coding Guide

Range of Addresses	Delivery Route
1000 - 9900 Solomon Lane 1- 500 Walker Road 50 -100 Western Street	A
9901 - 10000 Solomon Lane 101 - 500 Western Street	B
25 - 400 Crawley Ave. 1 - 200 Vernell Route 1 501 - 1000 Walker Road	C
All mail that doesn't fall in one of the address ranges listed above	D

	Delivery Address	Delivery Route				Answer Grid
1	1800 Solomon Lane	A	B	C	D	Ⓐ Ⓑ Ⓒ Ⓓ
2	345 Western Street	A	B	C	D	Ⓐ Ⓑ Ⓒ Ⓓ
3	400 Walker Road	A	B	C	D	Ⓐ Ⓑ Ⓒ Ⓓ
4	145 Vernell Route 1	A	B	C	D	Ⓐ Ⓑ Ⓒ Ⓓ
5	604 Walker Road	A	B	C	D	Ⓐ Ⓑ Ⓒ Ⓓ
6	68 Western Street	A	B	C	D	Ⓐ Ⓑ Ⓒ Ⓓ
7	9543 Solomon Lane	A	B	C	D	Ⓐ Ⓑ Ⓒ Ⓓ
8	1245 Walker Road	A	B	C	D	Ⓐ Ⓑ Ⓒ Ⓓ
9	178 Vernell Route 1	A	B	C	D	Ⓐ Ⓑ Ⓒ Ⓓ
10	498 Western Street	A	B	C	D	Ⓐ Ⓑ Ⓒ Ⓓ
11	470 Crawley Ave.	A	B	C	D	Ⓐ Ⓑ Ⓒ Ⓓ
12	398 Walker Road	A	B	C	D	Ⓐ Ⓑ Ⓒ Ⓓ
13	348 Vernell Route 1	A	B	C	D	Ⓐ Ⓑ Ⓒ Ⓓ
14	157 Crawley Ave.	A	B	C	D	Ⓐ Ⓑ Ⓒ Ⓓ

	Delivery Address	Delivery Route				Answer Grid
15	9860 Solomon Lane	A	B	C	D	Ⓐ Ⓑ Ⓒ Ⓓ
16	659 Walker Road	A	B	C	D	Ⓐ Ⓑ Ⓒ Ⓓ
17	1200 Solomon Lane	A	B	C	D	Ⓐ Ⓑ Ⓒ Ⓓ
18	56 Crawley Ave.	A	B	C	D	Ⓐ Ⓑ Ⓒ Ⓓ
19	34 Vernell Route 1	A	B	C	D	Ⓐ Ⓑ Ⓒ Ⓓ
20	345 Crawley Ave.	A	B	C	D	Ⓐ Ⓑ Ⓒ Ⓓ
21	224 Vernell Route 1	A	B	C	D	Ⓐ Ⓑ Ⓒ Ⓓ
22	95 Western Street	A	B	C	D	Ⓐ Ⓑ Ⓒ Ⓓ
23	9450 Solomon Lane	A	B	C	D	Ⓐ Ⓑ Ⓒ Ⓓ
24	895 Walker Road	A	B	C	D	Ⓐ Ⓑ Ⓒ Ⓓ
25	10901 Solomon Lane	A	B	C	D	Ⓐ Ⓑ Ⓒ Ⓓ
26	360 Western Street	A	B	C	D	Ⓐ Ⓑ Ⓒ Ⓓ
27	876 Crawley Ave.	A	B	C	D	Ⓐ Ⓑ Ⓒ Ⓓ
28	9000 Solomon Lane	A	B	C	D	Ⓐ Ⓑ Ⓒ Ⓓ
29	890 Walker Road	A	B	C	D	Ⓐ Ⓑ Ⓒ Ⓓ
30	30 Crawley Ave.	A	B	C	D	Ⓐ Ⓑ Ⓒ Ⓓ
31	2000 Walker Road	A	B	C	D	Ⓐ Ⓑ Ⓒ Ⓓ
32	67 Western Street	A	B	C	D	Ⓐ Ⓑ Ⓒ Ⓓ
33	67 Vernell Route 1	A	B	C	D	Ⓐ Ⓑ Ⓒ Ⓓ
34	505 Western Street	A	B	C	D	Ⓐ Ⓑ Ⓒ Ⓓ
35	256 Walker Road	A	B	C	D	Ⓐ Ⓑ Ⓒ Ⓓ
36	9750 Solomon Lane	A	B	C	D	Ⓐ Ⓑ Ⓒ Ⓓ

ANSWERS TO CODING EXERCISES

Coding Exercise #1

1. C	5. B	9. B	13. C	17. D	21. A	25. C	29. C	33. B
2. A	6. C	10. C	14. B	18. D	22. B	26. D	30. C	34. D
3. C	7. A	11. A	15. C	19. A	23. B	27. A	31. A	35. A
4. A	8. D	12. C	16. A	20. D	24. A	28. B	32. A	36. D

Coding Exercise #2

1. A	5. C	9. C	13. A	17. D	21. D	25. A	29. B	33. A
2. D	6. A	10. A	14. A	18. B	22. B	26. C	30. B	34. B
3. A	7. A	11. D	15. A	19. B	23. C	27. A	31. D	35. C
4. D	8. D	12. D	16. B	20. D	24. B	28. C	32. B	36. B

Coding Exercise #3

1. A	5. C	9. C	13. D	17. A	21. D	25. D	29. C	33. C
2. B	6. A	10. B	14. C	18. C	22. A	26. B	30. C	34. D
3. A	7. A	11. D	15. A	19. C	23. A	27. D	31. D	35. A
4. C	8. D	12. A	16. C	20. C	24. C	28. A	32. A	36. A

"Success depends upon previous preparation, and without such preparation there is sure to be failure."

-Confucius

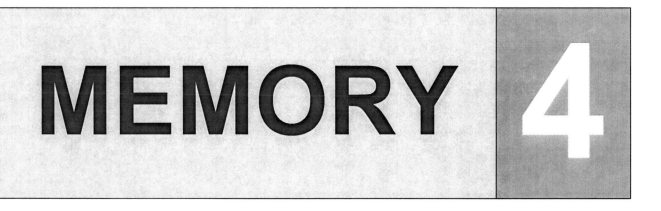

Part	Time Allowed	Number of Ques.	Description of Question
4. Memory (of coding examples, above)	7 minutes	36	Memorize address codes (which are same as codes in the "Coding" section part of the test.)

In the **MEMORY** part of the test you will be asked to determine the delivery routes of 36 addresses.

The coding guide will be the same as in the preceding coding questions section of the test.

HOWEVER, in MEMORY CODING you must determine the delivery routes by using your <u>MEMORY</u> of the coding guide.

In other words, you will **<u>not</u>** have the coding guide in front of you and you are not permitted to refer to it.

The coding guide will be the <u>same</u> coding guide that you will have used in the preceding coding section of the test.

One or two short sample coding sessions (which are not graded) may be provided for you to practice before you begin the actual coding by memory test.

During these practice examples (which may last for several minutes) you may want to memorize further the coding table.

Example of Coding Guide

Range of Addresses	Delivery Route
1 - 99 Rochester Avenue 100 - 1000 Bleeker Street 20 - 90 S. 18th Road	A
100 - 300 Rochester Avenue 91 - 200 S. 18th Road	B
5000 - 15000 Jefferson Lane 1 - 100 Rural Route 12 1001 - 5000 Bleeker Street	C
All mail that does not fall in one of address ranges listed above	D

Directions for the following 3 Coding By Memory Exercises

Each of the following 3 MEMORY exercises has 36 addresses which you must code by using your memory of the "Coding Guide" that is provided.

For each address, you will have to determine whether the address belongs to Delivery Route A, B, C or D, and mark your answer sheet accordingly.

You will be allowed 7 minutes to complete each of the following 3 coding exercises.

Note: On the actual test the MEMORY section will probably come right after the CODING section and you will already have had experience with the specific coding guide.

(The <u>same</u> coding guide is used for both the CODING and MEMORY sections.)

On the 3 practice tests in this book we will follow that pattern (CODING questions first and then MEMORY questions right after that.)

———————

However, for now and for study purposes, for the following 3 MEMORY exercises follow these instructions:

1. Allow yourself 5 minutes (like in the actual test) to memorize the coding guide.

2. After that, <u>cover the guide</u> and code the 36 addresses (A, B, C, D). (Allow yourself 7 minutes to code the 36 addresses.)

(Answers are on page 58.)

<u>Good Luck!</u>

Memory Exercise #1:   Coding Guide

Range of Addresses	Delivery Route
1 – 99 Ferndale Avenue 100 - 1000 Hazel Street 20 - 90 S. 12th Road	A
100 - 300 Ferndale Avenue 91 - 200 S. 12th Road	B
5000 - 15000 Lincoln Lane 1 - 100 Rural Route 2 1001 - 5000 Hazel Street	C
All mail that does not fall in one of address ranges listed above	D

		Delivery Address	Delivery Route				Answer Grid
	1	12000 Lincoln Lane	A	B	C	D	Ⓐ Ⓑ Ⓒ Ⓓ
	2	345 Hazel Street	A	B	C	D	Ⓐ Ⓑ Ⓒ Ⓓ
	3	79 S. 12th Road	A	B	C	D	Ⓐ Ⓑ Ⓒ Ⓓ
	4	20 Rural Route 2	A	B	C	D	Ⓐ Ⓑ Ⓒ Ⓓ
	5	25 Ferndale Avenue	A	B	C	D	Ⓐ Ⓑ Ⓒ Ⓓ
	6	6000 Hazel Street	A	B	C	D	Ⓐ Ⓑ Ⓒ Ⓓ
	7	95 S. 12th Road	A	B	C	D	Ⓐ Ⓑ Ⓒ Ⓓ
	8	290 Ferndale Avenue	A	B	C	D	Ⓐ Ⓑ Ⓒ Ⓓ
	9	11000 Lincoln Lane	A	B	C	D	Ⓐ Ⓑ Ⓒ Ⓓ
	10	2400 Rural Route 2	A	B	C	D	Ⓐ Ⓑ Ⓒ Ⓓ
	11	634 Hazel Street	A	B	C	D	Ⓐ Ⓑ Ⓒ Ⓓ
	12	50 Rural Route 2	A	B	C	D	Ⓐ Ⓑ Ⓒ Ⓓ
	13	400 Ferndale Avenue	A	B	C	D	Ⓐ Ⓑ Ⓒ Ⓓ
	14	260 S. 12th Road	A	B	C	D	Ⓐ Ⓑ Ⓒ Ⓓ

		Delivery Address	Delivery Route				Answer Grid
15		300 Ferndale Avenue	A	B	C	D	Ⓐ Ⓑ Ⓒ Ⓓ
16		76 Ferndale Avenue	A	B	C	D	Ⓐ Ⓑ Ⓒ Ⓓ
17		13000 Lincoln Lane	A	B	C	D	Ⓐ Ⓑ Ⓒ Ⓓ
18		24 Watkins Avenue	A	B	C	D	Ⓐ Ⓑ Ⓒ Ⓓ
19		240 Hazel Street	A	B	C	D	Ⓐ Ⓑ Ⓒ Ⓓ
20		2000 Hazel Street	A	B	C	D	Ⓐ Ⓑ Ⓒ Ⓓ
21		120 Ferndale Avenue	A	B	C	D	Ⓐ Ⓑ Ⓒ Ⓓ
22		76 S. 12th Road	A	B	C	D	Ⓐ Ⓑ Ⓒ Ⓓ
23		777 Ferndale Avenue	A	B	C	D	Ⓐ Ⓑ Ⓒ Ⓓ
24		75 Rural Route 2	A	B	C	D	Ⓐ Ⓑ Ⓒ Ⓓ
25		88 Ferndale Avenue	A	B	C	D	Ⓐ Ⓑ Ⓒ Ⓓ
26		150 S. 12th Road	A	B	C	D	Ⓐ Ⓑ Ⓒ Ⓓ
27		5500 Lincoln Lane	A	B	C	D	Ⓐ Ⓑ Ⓒ Ⓓ
28		600 Albert Lane	A	B	C	D	Ⓐ Ⓑ Ⓒ Ⓓ
29		800 Hazel Street	A	B	C	D	Ⓐ Ⓑ Ⓒ Ⓓ
30		6500 Hazel Street	A	B	C	D	Ⓐ Ⓑ Ⓒ Ⓓ
31		168 Ferndale Avenue	A	B	C	D	Ⓐ Ⓑ Ⓒ Ⓓ
32		4000 Hazel Street	A	B	C	D	Ⓐ Ⓑ Ⓒ Ⓓ
33		60 S. 12th Road	A	B	C	D	Ⓐ Ⓑ Ⓒ Ⓓ
34		95 Rural Route 2	A	B	C	D	Ⓐ Ⓑ Ⓒ Ⓓ
35		52 Ferndale Avenue	A	B	C	D	Ⓐ Ⓑ Ⓒ Ⓓ
36		6100 Lincoln Lane	A	B	C	D	Ⓐ Ⓑ Ⓒ Ⓓ

Memory Exercise #2: Coding Guide

Range of Addresses	Delivery Route
1 - 49 Western Lane 200 - 900 Jennings Street 25 - 75 North Circle	A
50 - 200 Western Lane 76 - 200 North Circle	B
100 - 1200 King Ave. 1 - 100 Furman Route 10 901 - 1000 Jennings Street	C
All mail that doesn't fall in one of the address ranges listed above	D

	Delivery Address	Delivery Route				Answer Grid
1	25 Western Lane	A	B	C	D	Ⓐ Ⓑ Ⓒ Ⓓ
2	77 North Circle	A	B	C	D	Ⓐ Ⓑ Ⓒ Ⓓ
3	50 Western Lane	A	B	C	D	Ⓐ Ⓑ Ⓒ Ⓓ
4	45 Furman Route 10	A	B	C	D	Ⓐ Ⓑ Ⓒ Ⓓ
5	748 Jennings Street	A	B	C	D	Ⓐ Ⓑ Ⓒ Ⓓ
6	125 King Ave.	A	B	C	D	Ⓐ Ⓑ Ⓒ Ⓓ
7	990 Jennings Street	A	B	C	D	Ⓐ Ⓑ Ⓒ Ⓓ
8	55 North Circle	A	B	C	D	Ⓐ Ⓑ Ⓒ Ⓓ
9	88 Furman Route 10	A	B	C	D	Ⓐ Ⓑ Ⓒ Ⓓ
10	22 Western Lane	A	B	C	D	Ⓐ Ⓑ Ⓒ Ⓓ
11	220 Western Lane	A	B	C	D	Ⓐ Ⓑ Ⓒ Ⓓ
12	105 North Circle	A	B	C	D	Ⓐ Ⓑ Ⓒ Ⓓ
13	980 Jennings Street	A	B	C	D	Ⓐ Ⓑ Ⓒ Ⓓ
14	75 North Circle	A	B	C	D	Ⓐ Ⓑ Ⓒ Ⓓ

	Delivery Address	Delivery Route				Answer Grid
15	500 Jennings Street	A	B	C	D	Ⓐ Ⓑ Ⓒ Ⓓ
16	1200 Jennings Street	A	B	C	D	Ⓐ Ⓑ Ⓒ Ⓓ
17	150 Western Lane	A	B	C	D	Ⓐ Ⓑ Ⓒ Ⓓ
18	85 Furman Route 10	A	B	C	D	Ⓐ Ⓑ Ⓒ Ⓓ
19	30 North Circle	A	B	C	D	Ⓐ Ⓑ Ⓒ Ⓓ
20	940 Jennings Street	A	B	C	D	Ⓐ Ⓑ Ⓒ Ⓓ
21	45 Western Lane	A	B	C	D	Ⓐ Ⓑ Ⓒ Ⓓ
22	50 King Avenue	A	B	C	D	Ⓐ Ⓑ Ⓒ Ⓓ
23	600 King Ave.	A	B	C	D	Ⓐ Ⓑ Ⓒ Ⓓ
24	325 Jennings Street	A	B	C	D	Ⓐ Ⓑ Ⓒ Ⓓ
25	215 North Circle	A	B	C	D	Ⓐ Ⓑ Ⓒ Ⓓ
26	169 North Circle	A	B	C	D	Ⓐ Ⓑ Ⓒ Ⓓ
27	800 Bedford Avenue	A	B	C	D	Ⓐ Ⓑ Ⓒ Ⓓ
28	632 Jennings Street	A	B	C	D	Ⓐ Ⓑ Ⓒ Ⓓ
29	16 Wilkes Road	A	B	C	D	Ⓐ Ⓑ Ⓒ Ⓓ
30	190 Western Lane	A	B	C	D	Ⓐ Ⓑ Ⓒ Ⓓ
31	46 Furman Route 10	A	B	C	D	Ⓐ Ⓑ Ⓒ Ⓓ
32	105 Western Lane	A	B	C	D	Ⓐ Ⓑ Ⓒ Ⓓ
33	778 King Ave.	A	B	C	D	Ⓐ Ⓑ Ⓒ Ⓓ
34	1800 Jennings Street	A	B	C	D	Ⓐ Ⓑ Ⓒ Ⓓ
35	40 Western Lane	A	B	C	D	Ⓐ Ⓑ Ⓒ Ⓓ
36	97 North Circle	A	B	C	D	Ⓐ Ⓑ Ⓒ Ⓓ

Memory Exercise #3:   Coding Guide

Range of Addresses	Delivery Route
1000 – 9900 Solomon Lane 1 - 500 Walker Road 50 -100 Western Street	A
9901 – 10000 Solomon Lane 101 - 500 Western Street	B
25 – 400 Crawley Ave. 1 – 200 Vernell Route 1 501 – 1000 Walker Road	C
All mail that doesn't fall in one of the address ranges listed above	D

	Delivery Address	Delivery Route				Answer Grid
1	400 Walker Road	A	B	C	D	Ⓐ Ⓑ Ⓒ Ⓓ
2	2000 Walker Road	A	B	C	D	Ⓐ Ⓑ Ⓒ Ⓓ
3	50 Western Street	A	B	C	D	Ⓐ Ⓑ Ⓒ Ⓓ
4	30 Crawley Ave.	A	B	C	D	Ⓐ Ⓑ Ⓒ Ⓓ
5	500 Crawley Ave.	A	B	C	D	Ⓐ Ⓑ Ⓒ Ⓓ
6	2055 Solomon Lane	A	B	C	D	Ⓐ Ⓑ Ⓒ Ⓓ
7	9910 Solomon Lane	A	B	C	D	Ⓐ Ⓑ Ⓒ Ⓓ
8	650 Walker Road	A	B	C	D	Ⓐ Ⓑ Ⓒ Ⓓ
9	75 Western Street	A	B	C	D	Ⓐ Ⓑ Ⓒ Ⓓ
10	105 Vernell Route 1	A	B	C	D	Ⓐ Ⓑ Ⓒ Ⓓ
11	9950 Solomon Lane	A	B	C	D	Ⓐ Ⓑ Ⓒ Ⓓ
12	800 Crawley Ave.	A	B	C	D	Ⓐ Ⓑ Ⓒ Ⓓ
13	488 Walker Road	A	B	C	D	Ⓐ Ⓑ Ⓒ Ⓓ
14	360 Western Street	A	B	C	D	Ⓐ Ⓑ Ⓒ Ⓓ

	Delivery Address	Delivery Route				Answer Grid
15	5400 Solomon Lane	A	B	C	D	Ⓐ Ⓑ Ⓒ Ⓓ
16	32 Crawley Ave.	A	B	C	D	Ⓐ Ⓑ Ⓒ Ⓓ
17	850 Abington Road	A	B	C	D	Ⓐ Ⓑ Ⓒ Ⓓ
18	470 Walker Road	A	B	C	D	Ⓐ Ⓑ Ⓒ Ⓓ
19	9989 Solomon Lane	A	B	C	D	Ⓐ Ⓑ Ⓒ Ⓓ
20	69 Western Street	A	B	C	D	Ⓐ Ⓑ Ⓒ Ⓓ
21	932 Walker Road	A	B	C	D	Ⓐ Ⓑ Ⓒ Ⓓ
22	10 Vernell Route 1	A	B	C	D	Ⓐ Ⓑ Ⓒ Ⓓ
23	2000 Solomon Lane	A	B	C	D	Ⓐ Ⓑ Ⓒ Ⓓ
24	700 Walker Road	A	B	C	D	Ⓐ Ⓑ Ⓒ Ⓓ
25	125 Western Street	A	B	C	D	Ⓐ Ⓑ Ⓒ Ⓓ
26	9990 Solomon Lane	A	B	C	D	Ⓐ Ⓑ Ⓒ Ⓓ
27	476 Western Street	A	B	C	D	Ⓐ Ⓑ Ⓒ Ⓓ
28	900 Hampton Road	A	B	C	D	Ⓐ Ⓑ Ⓒ Ⓓ
29	325 Walker Road	A	B	C	D	Ⓐ Ⓑ Ⓒ Ⓓ
30	370 Crawley Ave.	A	B	C	D	Ⓐ Ⓑ Ⓒ Ⓓ
31	88 Pimrose Street	A	B	C	D	Ⓐ Ⓑ Ⓒ Ⓓ
32	56 Vernell Route 1	A	B	C	D	Ⓐ Ⓑ Ⓒ Ⓓ
33	3000 Walker Road	A	B	C	D	Ⓐ Ⓑ Ⓒ Ⓓ
34	99 Western Street	A	B	C	D	Ⓐ Ⓑ Ⓒ Ⓓ
35	800 Walker Road	A	B	C	D	Ⓐ Ⓑ Ⓒ Ⓓ
36	8600 Solomon Lane	A	B	C	D	Ⓐ Ⓑ Ⓒ Ⓓ

Answers to Memory Coding Exercises

Exercise #1

1. C	5. A	9. C	13. D	17. C	21. B	25. A	29. A	33. A
2. A	6. D	10. D	14. D	18. D	22. A	26. B	30. D	34. C
3. A	7. B	11. A	15. B	19. A	23. D	27. C	31. B	35. A
4. C	8. B	12. C	16. A	20. C	24. C	28. D	32. C	36. C

Exercise #2

1. A	5. A	9. C	13. C	17. B	21. A	25. D	29. D	33. C
2. B	6. C	10. A	14. A	18. C	22. D	26. B	30. B	34. D
3. B	7. C	11. D	15. A	19. A	23. C	27. D	31. C	35. A
4. C	8. A	12. B	16. D	20. C	24. A	28. A	32. B	36. B

Exercise #3

1. A	5. D	9. A	13. A	17. D	21. C	25. B	29. A	33. D
2. D	6. A	10. C	14. B	18. A	22. C	26. B	30. C	34. A
3. A	7. B	11. B	15. A	19. B	23. A	27. B	31. D	35. C
4. C	8. C	12. D	16. C	20. A	24. C	28. D	32. C	36. A

"The first requisite of success is the ability to apply your physical and mental energies to one problem without growing weary."

-Thomas Edison

PERSONAL CHARACTERISTICS AND EXPERIENCE INVENTORY

Part	Time Allowed	Number of Ques.	Description of Question
5. Personal Characteristics and Experience Inventory	90 minutes	236	Tests for experience and job-related tendencies.

Would you ask someone to play basketball with you if you knew that he did not like the game?

Would you ask someone to see a movie with you if you knew that he did not like that particular movie?

Of course not.

If you were an employer, would you want to hire someone who did not like to work?

Would you hire someone who admitted that he could never get out of bed and was therefore frequently late?

Of course not.

The United States Postal Service has to be very careful that the employees it hires have the <u>right attitude, motivation, and psychological state</u> to help them succeed in their work.

According to the USPS, the personal characteristics and experience inventory questions can be classified into 3 types:

    1. Questions that call for an Agree/Disagree answer.

    2. Questions that ask the frequency of something.

    3. Questions that relate to your experience.

<u>**Examples**</u>

1. Questions that call for an <u>Agree/Disagree answer</u>.

I always like to work alone.

A. Strongly agree

B. Agree

C. Disagree

D. Strongly disagree

---

2. Questions that ask the <u>frequency of something</u>.

I become angry if I have to work overtime.

A. Very often

B. Often

C. Sometimes

D. Rarely

3. Questions that <u>relate to your experience</u>.

What type of a supervisor would you like the least?

A. a supervisor who is younger than me

B. a supervisor who is older than me

C. a supervisor who is more knowledgeable than me

D. a female supervisor

E. a male supervisor

F. would not mind any of the above supervisors

G. I am not sure.

Your <u>appropriate and reasonable</u> responses to these questions are evaluated to help determine whether or not you are a suitable candidate for employment with the postal service.

Because there are no strict "right" or "wrong" answers, practicing these types of questions is not advisable.

PRACTICE TESTS

The Postal test 473E consists of 5 parts:

    1. Address Checking

    2. Forms Completion

    3. Coding

    4. Memory

    5. Personal Characteristics and Experience Inventory

In the following 3 practice tests you will practice test sections 1 – 4.

Each section is timed. (You are only allowed to work on the questions in that part during the allotted time. You **cannot** go to questions from a different part.)

Part	Time Allowed	Number of Ques.	Description of Question
1. Address Checking	11 minutes	60	Compare two addresses.
2. Forms Completion	15 minutes	30	Correctly complete forms.
3. Coding	6 minutes	36	Find correct code for an address.
4. Memory (of coding examples, above)	7 minutes	36	Memorize address codes (which are same as codes in the "Coding" section part of the test.)
5. Personal Characteristics and Experience Inventory	90 minutes	236	Tests for experience and job-related tendencies.

When you practice with these tests, try to simulate test conditions:

1. Find a quiet place where you will not be interrupted.

2. Follow the time allowed directions carefully (STOP at the end of the allotted time.)

3. Try to complete sections 1 – 4 for each test at one sitting.

PRACTICE TEST

Part	Time Allowed	Number of Ques.	Description of Question
1. Address Checking	**11 minutes**	**60**	**Compare two addresses.**
2. Forms Completion	15 minutes	30	Correctly complete forms.
3. Coding	6 minutes	36	Find correct code for an address.
4. Memory (of coding examples, above)	7 minutes	36	Memorize address codes (which are same as codes in the "Coding" section part of the test.)

The first Part of this practice test is ADDRESS CHECKING.

(You have 11 minutes to complete this part of the test.)

When you are ready, turn the page and start the test.

———

FREE INTERACTIVE Access Code for PostalTest.com website is: 437347

Address Checking Practice Test 1: Below are 60 pairs of addresses. You have 11 minutes to compare each pair for errors and mark the answer sheet to indicate errors found as follows:

A. No Errors   **B.** Address Only   **C.** Zip Code Only   **D.** Both Address and ZIP Code

	Correct List of Addresses		Address List to be Checked		
	Address	**ZIP**	**Address**	**ZIP**	**Answer Grid**
1	73 Commers Ave. Norman, VA	32195	73 Comers Ave. Norman, VA	32195	Ⓐ Ⓑ Ⓒ Ⓓ
2	525 Island Cir. Misnsky, NY	78921-2114	525 Island Cir. Misnsky, NY	78921-2114	Ⓐ Ⓑ Ⓒ Ⓓ
3	8985 Liberty Ln. Lola, FL	40558	8935 Liberty Ln. Lola, FL	40523	Ⓐ Ⓑ Ⓒ Ⓓ
4	2571 Carson St. Paradise, AK	33843-0208	2571 Carson St. Paradise, AK	33843-0208	Ⓐ Ⓑ Ⓒ Ⓓ
5	1837 Jones Road Beidly, FL	80562-0208	1887 Jones Road Beidly, FL	80562-0208	Ⓐ Ⓑ Ⓒ Ⓓ
6	690 Keller Lane Poplar, IL	41504-7421	690 Keller Lane Poplar, IL	41504-7421	Ⓐ Ⓑ Ⓒ Ⓓ
7	7831 Forest Ct. Kings, MI	74857	7831 Forest Ct. Kings, MI	74857	Ⓐ Ⓑ Ⓒ Ⓓ
8	4932 Holms Way Questor, MN	34685	4932 Holms Way Questor, MN	34985	Ⓐ Ⓑ Ⓒ Ⓓ
9	987 Justice St. Elk, CT	10501-7463	9887 Justice St Elk, CT	10501-1463	Ⓐ Ⓑ Ⓒ Ⓓ
10	564 Caraco Ave. Davin, CT	74630	564 Caraco Ave. Davin, CT	74630	Ⓐ Ⓑ Ⓒ Ⓓ
11	318 Mecal Pkwy. Kalb, TX	39205	378 Mecal Pkwy. Kalb, TX	39205	Ⓐ Ⓑ Ⓒ Ⓓ
12	1516 Roller Lane Corier, MA	04172-3143	1516 Roller Lane Corier, MA	04175-3143	Ⓐ Ⓑ Ⓒ Ⓓ
13	60 Butler Rd. Tandy, WA	90211	60 Butler Rd. Tandy, WA	98211	Ⓐ Ⓑ Ⓒ Ⓓ
14	P.O. Box 2044 Manor, WA	40382-2354	P.O. Box 2044 Manor, WA	40382-2354	Ⓐ Ⓑ Ⓒ Ⓓ
15	7824 Danfill Ter. Livingston, CA	09365-1014	7824 Danfil Ter. Livingston, CA	09365-1014	Ⓐ Ⓑ Ⓒ Ⓓ

Address Checking Practice Test 1 (cont'd): Continue to compare each pair of addresses for errors and mark the answer sheet as follows:

A. No Errors   **B.** Address Only   **C.** Zip Code Only   **D.** Both Address and ZIP Code

	Correct List of Addresses		Address List to be Checked		
	Address	**ZIP**	**Address**	**ZIP**	**Answer Grid**
16	667 Point Ln. Akron, MN	56802-3182	667 Point Ln. Akron, MA	56802-3782	Ⓐ Ⓑ Ⓒ Ⓓ
17	P.O. Box 3109 Pelham, AR	54410-4172	P.O. Box 3106 Pelham, AR	54410-4172	Ⓐ Ⓑ Ⓒ Ⓓ
18	3317 Church St. Midland, MA	85745	3317 Church St. Midland, MA	85745	Ⓐ Ⓑ Ⓒ Ⓓ
19	1762 West 18th St. Helena, CT	68845	1762 East 18th St. Helena, CT	68345	Ⓐ Ⓑ Ⓒ Ⓓ
20	4259 Kotter Ave. Kinsey, ME	7012-4613	4259 Kotter Ave. Kinsey, ME	7012-4613	Ⓐ Ⓑ Ⓒ Ⓓ
21	2183 Delroy Cir. Brenton, FL	43760	2183 Delroy Cir. Brenton, FL	43160	Ⓐ Ⓑ Ⓒ Ⓓ
22	7287 Benson Way Elba, MS	25390	7287 Benson Way Elby, MS	25390	Ⓐ Ⓑ Ⓒ Ⓓ
23	3639 Kawanis Rd. Heflin, MN	73010-4644	3639 Kawanis Rd. Heflin, MN	73010-4644	Ⓐ Ⓑ Ⓒ Ⓓ
24	54 Campfield Rd. Cardiff, IL	29110	54 Campfield Rd. Cardiff, IL	59110	Ⓐ Ⓑ Ⓒ Ⓓ
25	1620 Charles St. Newton, OR	38402-4224	1920 Charles St. Newton, OR	38402-4234	Ⓐ Ⓑ Ⓒ Ⓓ
26	4182 Stock Ave. Grant, NY	36096-0204	4182 Stock Ave. Grant, NY	36096-0204	Ⓐ Ⓑ Ⓒ Ⓓ
27	716 Riverdale Ct. Dozier, AR	43011-9127	116 Riverdale Ct. Dozier, AR	43011-9127	Ⓐ Ⓑ Ⓒ Ⓓ
28	868 Country Lane Elberta, MI	38978	863 Country Lane Elberta, MI	38918	Ⓐ Ⓑ Ⓒ Ⓓ
29	384 Best Terrace Samson, SC	24117-3491	384 Best Terrace Samson, SC	24117-3491	Ⓐ Ⓑ Ⓒ Ⓓ
30	514 Asalon Pkwy. Calera, CA	10204	514 Azalon Pkwy. Calera, CA	10204	Ⓐ Ⓑ Ⓒ Ⓓ

Address Checking Practice Test 1 (cont'd): Continue to compare each pair of addresses for errors and mark the answer sheet as follows:

A. No Errors   **B.** Address Only   **C.** Zip Code Only   **D.** Both Address and ZIP Code

	Correct List of Addresses		Address List to be Checked		
	Address	**ZIP**	**Address**	**ZIP**	**Answer Grid**
31	1689 Burnet St. Oxford, OH	26028-1948	1687 Burnet St. Oxford, OH	26023-1948	A B C D
32	81 Seneg Pkwy. Madrid, OH	97522	81 Seneg Pkwy. Madrid, AK	97522	A B C D
33	6133 Century St. Dayton, AK	92697	6133 Century St. Dayton, AK	92697	A B C D
34	3658 Placid Rd. Idler, MD	19048-9347	365 Placid Rd. Idler, MD	19048-9341	A B C D
35	8782 Conner Ave. Dora, WA	94897-9746	8782 Coner Ave. Dora, WA	94897-9746	A B C D
36	226 Junior Cir. Brent, RI	26137-6254	226 Junior Cir. Brent, RI	26137-6254	A B C D
37	4748 Point St. Hoover, PA	18247	4748 Point St. Hoover, PA	18547	A B C D
38	1000 Collins Ave. Grimes, VA	19232-9783	100 Collins Ave. Grimes, VA	19232-9183	A B C D
39	286 Rainbow Ct. Argo, ME	24563	286 Rainbow Ct. Argo, ME	24568	A B C D
40	4519 Ridge Way Auburn, KS	13102-1265	4519 Ridge Way Auburn, KS	13102-1265	A B C D
41	721 Veteran Ln. Centre, NY	54258	721 Veterans Ln. Centre, NY	54758	A B C D
42	P.O. Box 9183 Geiger, WA	19325	P.O. Box 9183 Geiger, WA	19322	A B C D
43	946 Tourist Rd. Leeds, NJ	92782-1372	9463 Tourist Rd. Leeds, NJ	92782-1312	A B C D
44	3121 Master Ave. Lincoln, MI	52403	312 Master Ave. Lincoln, MI	55403	A B C D
45	1629 Eastern Ln. Florence, TX	83134-0103	1629 Eastern Ln. Florence, TX	83134-0103	A B C D

Address Checking Practice Test 1 (cont'd): Continue to compare each pair of addresses for errors and mark the answer sheet as follows:

A. No Errors   **B.** Address Only   **C.** Zip Code Only   **D.** Both Address and ZIP Code

	Correct List of Addresses		Address List to be Checked		
	Address	ZIP	Address	ZIP	Answer Grid
46	3317 China Street Seward, MO	05354	3317 China Street Seward, MO	05324	A B C D
47	8159 Brinks Lane Tanker, VA	38433-0201	859 Brinks Lane Tanker, VA	38433-2001	A B C D
48	114 Rockaway Ct. Youngs, NY	05268-8372	114 Rockaway Ct. Youngs, NY	05268-8375	A B C D
49	2090 Hatter Ave. Vance, WA	15044-7412	2090 Hater Ave. Vance, WA	15044-7412	A B C D
50	3162 Overton Rd. Williams, MD	48557	362 Overton Rd. Williams, MD	48527	A B C D
51	6274 North Way Ruby, NJ	46583	6274 North Way Ruby, NY	46583	A B C D
52	567 Memorial Ln. Larsen, KS	64073	567 Memorial Ln. Larsen, KS	64013	A B C D
53	711 Reves Pkwy. Adak, SC	07210-1436	771 Reves Pkwy. Adak, SC	07210-1436	A B C D
54	4683 Clinton St. Kodiak, PA	92053	4683 Clinton St. Kodiak, PA	92058	A B C D
55	2716 Meteor Cir. St. Paul, MN	17030-6432	2716 Meteor Cir. St. Paul, MN	17080-6432	A B C D
56	3241 Colonial Ave. Monroe, RI	15090	324 Colonial Ave. Monroe, RI	12090	A B C D
57	P.O. Box 7882 Barrow, TX	03284-3524	P.O. Box 7382 Barrow, TX	03284-3524	A B C D
58	4553 Broad Rd. Craig, ME	93660-1089	4553 Broad Rd. Craig, ME	93660-1039	A B C D
59	479 Power Street Willow, AK	44001-2917	479 Power Street Willow, AK	44001-2917	A B C D
60	924 North Terrace Waldez, OH	13889	924 North Terrace Waldez, OR	13889	A B C D

Forms Completion Practice Test 1

This part of the test consists of 5 different forms and 30 questions relating to the 5 forms. Study each form and then answer the questions following each of the forms. (Time allowed: 15 minutes for 30 questions).

Answer questions 1 – 6 based on the following form:

1. RECEIPT FOR INSURED MAIL		
15.	2. Postage	6. ☐ Fragile 7. ☐ Perishable
		8. ☐ Liquid 9. ☐ Hazardous
	3. Insurance Fee	10.
		11. Stamp Postmark Here
	4. Handling Fee	
	5. Total (Postage plus Fees) $_____	
12. Addressee (Sent to):		
13. Street, Apt. Number; or PO Box Number		
14. City, State and ZIP		

	Question	Answer Grid
1	The postmark should be stamped in box: A. 2 B. 15 C. 10 D. 11	Ⓐ Ⓑ Ⓒ Ⓓ
2	The name of the person to whom the mail is being sent should be written in box: A. 15 B. 11 C. 12 D. 10	Ⓐ Ⓑ Ⓒ Ⓓ
3	Where on this form should the ZIP number of the addressee be entered? A. 11 B. 14 C. 3 D. 13	Ⓐ Ⓑ Ⓒ Ⓓ
4	The mail includes fresh pears that are perishable. This should be indicated by a checkmark in box: A. 2 B. 4 C. 7 D. 6	Ⓐ Ⓑ Ⓒ Ⓓ
5	The address of addressee includes "21 West Street." This should be recorded in box: A. 11 B. 8 C. 13 D. 14	Ⓐ Ⓑ Ⓒ Ⓓ
6	David Kim, a Postal Clerk, processes this receipt. He should sign his name in box: A. 15 B. 12 C. 11 D. He should not sign his name.	Ⓐ Ⓑ Ⓒ Ⓓ

(Answers for Test 1 are on page 82.)

Answer questions 7 – 12 based on the following form:

1. RETURN RECEIPT FOR DOMESTIC MAIL		
THIS WHITE SECTION IS TO BE COMPLETED BY THE SENDER	**THIS DARK SECTION IS TO BE COMPLETED UPON DELIVERY OF THE ITEM**	
2. ►Sender must complete items 5, 6, 12, 13, 14, 15, 16, 17 (and 18 if Restricted Delivery is desired.) 3. ►Sender must print sender's name and address on the reverse side of this card so that card can be returned to sender. 4. ►Peel off glue protector strips on opposite side and attach to the back of the mail, or on the front if there is enough space.	7. Signature ►	□ Addressee □ Agent
	8. Received by (PRINT)	9. Delivery Date
	10. Is delivery address same or different from item 5? □ Same □ Different (If different, write delivery address below:	
5. Article addressed to:	Type of mail service:	
	12. □ Registered	15. □ C.O.D.
	13. □ Insured	16. □ Express
	14. □ Certified	17. □ Merchandise Return receipt
	18. Restricted delivery (Additional fee) $_____ □ Yes	
6. Article number (from service label)		

Question	Answer Grid
7 The sender should complete all of the following boxes, except box: A. 5 B. 12 C. 6 D. 7	Ⓐ Ⓑ Ⓒ Ⓓ
8 Upon receipt of the mail, the recipient should sign in box: A. 6 B. 8 C. 7 D. 5	Ⓐ Ⓑ Ⓒ Ⓓ
9 Where on this form should the ZIP number of the person to whom mail is addressed be entered? A. 5 B. 6 C. 8 D. 7	Ⓐ Ⓑ Ⓒ Ⓓ
10 If restricted delivery is requested, that information should be recorded in box: A. 5 B. 7 C. 12 D. 18	Ⓐ Ⓑ Ⓒ Ⓓ
11 The service label has the article number "3864952978." This information should be recorded in box: A. 5 B. 6 C. 14 D. 12	Ⓐ Ⓑ Ⓒ Ⓓ
12 If the delivery address is the same as from item 5, in which box should this be indicated? A. 10 B. 11 C. 18 D. 6	Ⓐ Ⓑ Ⓒ Ⓓ

(Answers for Test 1 are on page 82.)

Answer questions 13 – 18 based on the following form:

STATEMENT FOR PICKUP SERVICE			
1. Information (Product)		**2. Information (Customer)**	
Type of pickup service	**Quantity**	13. First and Last Name	
3. Priority Mail	8.	14. Company Name	
4. Express Mail	9.	15. Address 1.	
5. Parcel Post	10.	16. Address 2	
6.Global Express Guaranteed	11.	17. City	
		18. State.	
7. Estimated weight (total) of all packages (in pounds)	12.	19. Zip + 4	
29.			
20. Affix stamps or Meter Strip in this space		**Method of Payment**	
		21. □ Metered Postage or Stamps	
		22. □ Postage Due Account	
		23. □ Express Mail Corporate Account Number	
		24. □ Check (Payable to Postmaster)	
		25. □ Label For Merchandise Return	
26. Signature of Customer	27. Signature of USPS employee		28. Pickup Date and Time

	Question	Answer Grid
13	The postal employee should sign in which box? A. 20　　　　B. 13　　　　C. 27　　　　D. 29	Ⓐ Ⓑ Ⓒ Ⓓ
14	The number of Express Mail items picked up is indicated in box: A. 29　　　　B. 12　　　　C. 3　　　　D. 9	Ⓐ Ⓑ Ⓒ Ⓓ
15	Payment is made with postage stamps. The stamps should be affixed in box: A. 21　　　　B. 20　　　　C. 22　　　　D. 29	Ⓐ Ⓑ Ⓒ Ⓓ
16	If payment is made by check, a checkmark should be placed in box: A. 19　　　　B. 6　　　　C. 24　　　　D. 16	Ⓐ Ⓑ Ⓒ Ⓓ
17	If payment is made by check, it must be made payable to: A. USPS Clerk　　B. Postmaster　　C. Carrier　　　D. Cash	Ⓐ Ⓑ Ⓒ Ⓓ
18	Which of the following is a correct entry for box 12? A. 14 kg.　　　　B. 11 lbs.　　　C. 8 pints　　　D. 19 gm.	Ⓐ Ⓑ Ⓒ Ⓓ

(Answers for Test 1 are on page 82.)

Answer questions 19 – 24 based on the following form:

CUSTOMS DECLARATION	
FROM (SENDER): 1. Last and First Name (and Business Name, if any) 2. Street 3. City 4. State 5. Zip	11. Insured Amount
	12. Insured Fees (U.S. $)
	13. Importer's Name and Telephone Number

TO (ADDRESSEE):
6. Last and First Name (and Business Name, if any)
 	
7. Street
 	
8. City
 	
9. State   10. Zip
	14. Sender's instructions in case cannot be delivered:
	15. □ Treat as abandoned
	    □ Return to sender
	    □ Redirect to following address (#16):
	16.

17. Specific description of contents	18. Qty	19. Lbs.	20. Oz.
21. Comments			
22. Check one 23. □ Airmail/Priority 24. □ Surface/Non priority			
25. Check one 26. □ Documents 27. □ Merchandise 28. □ Gift 29. □ Other _____			
30. Date Signed 31. Sender's Signature			

Question	Answer Grid
19 The contents of the article is "Children's books." This information should be recorded in box: A. 15 B. 16 C. 17 D. 18	(A) (B) (C) (D)
20 The customer wishes this article to be shipped by Airmail. This should be indicated with a checkmark in box: A. 15 B. 26 C. 27 D. 23	(A) (B) (C) (D)
21 Where on this form should the ZIP number of the addressee be entered? A. 5 B. 7 C. 4 D. 10	(A) (B) (C) (D)
22 The insured amount is $325.00. This should be recorded in box: A. 12 B. 11 C. 29 D. 16	(A) (B) (C) (D)
23 The customer signed this form on 11/22/2010. This date should be written in box: A. 18 B. 19 C. 30 D. 7	(A) (B) (C) (D)
24 The contents weigh 6 pounds. The number "6" should be written in box: A. 18 B. 19 C. 30 D. 20	(A) (B) (C) (D)

(Answers for Test 1 are on page 82.)

Answer questions 25 – 30 based on the following form:

Application for Nonprofit Standard Mail Prices	
1. Legal Name of Organization	2. Street Address (including Street/Suite Number)
	3. City, State, Zip
4. Telephone	5. E-mail address
6. Alternate mailing address (if any)	
Type of Organization (Check only one box) 7. □ Educational 8. □ Religious 9. □ Scientific 10. □ Labor 11. □ Veterans	
12. Has this organization previously mailed at nonprofit standard prices? 13. □ YES 14. □ NO	15. If the answer to 12 is "YES", have standard mail privileges ever been revoked? 16. □ YES 17. □ NO
18. Signature of applicant	19. Title of applicant
20. Date this request is submitted.	

	Question	Answer Grid
25	The name of the person requesting Nonprofit Standard Mail Prices is "William Bentley." He should sign in box: A. 1 B. 2 C. 10 D. 18	Ⓐ Ⓑ Ⓒ Ⓓ
26	The applicant "William Bentley" is the president of ABC Charities, Inc. He should write "President" in box: A. 18 B. 19 C. 1 D. 5	Ⓐ Ⓑ Ⓒ Ⓓ

27	The fact that this organization previously mailed at nonprofit standard prices must be indicated by checking box: A. 14 B. 19 C. 13 D. 6	Ⓐ Ⓑ Ⓒ Ⓓ
28	The date that this request is submitted should be indicated in box: A. 19 B. 6 C. 1 D. 20	Ⓐ Ⓑ Ⓒ Ⓓ
29	The postal service received the form on 9/25/10. This date should be recorded in box: A. 19 B. 8 C. 20 D. 7	Ⓐ Ⓑ Ⓒ Ⓓ
30	The applicant's charitable company, "ABC Charities, Inc." is a religious organization. Which box should be checked to indicate the type of organization? A. 14 B. 11 C. 8 D. 19	Ⓐ Ⓑ Ⓒ Ⓓ

Directions for the 36 Coding Questions
on the following page:

For each of the following 36 "Delivery Addresses" determine based on the coding guide whether the address belongs to Delivery Route A, B, C or D, and mark your answer grid accordingly. You have 6 minutes to code the 36 addresses.

Coding Practice Test #1:   Coding Guide

Range of Addresses	Delivery Route
100 – 999 Elton Parkway 1 - 200 Walters Ave. 50 - 150 N. 32nd Street	A
1000 – 2000 Elton Parkway 151 – 300 N. 32nd Street	B
500 – 6000 Veronica Ave. 1 – 1000 Victory Blvd. 201 – 1500 Walters Ave.	C
All mail that doesn't fall in one of the address ranges listed above	D

	Delivery Address	Delivery Route				Answer Grid
1	161 N. 32nd Street	A	B	C	D	Ⓐ Ⓑ Ⓒ Ⓓ
2	150 Elton Parkway	A	B	C	D	Ⓐ Ⓑ Ⓒ Ⓓ
3	510 Veronica Ave.	A	B	C	D	Ⓐ Ⓑ Ⓒ Ⓓ
4	125 Walters Ave.	A	B	C	D	Ⓐ Ⓑ Ⓒ Ⓓ
5	1000 Elton Parkway	A	B	C	D	Ⓐ Ⓑ Ⓒ Ⓓ
6	201 Walters Ave.	A	B	C	D	Ⓐ Ⓑ Ⓒ Ⓓ
7	195 Walters Ave.	A	B	C	D	Ⓐ Ⓑ Ⓒ Ⓓ
8	100 Victory Blvd.	A	B	C	D	Ⓐ Ⓑ Ⓒ Ⓓ
9	900 Elton Parkway	A	B	C	D	Ⓐ Ⓑ Ⓒ Ⓓ
10	245 Bradford Ave.	A	B	C	D	Ⓐ Ⓑ Ⓒ Ⓓ
11	50 N. 32nd Street	A	B	C	D	Ⓐ Ⓑ Ⓒ Ⓓ
12	1820 Wycoff Street	A	B	C	D	Ⓐ Ⓑ Ⓒ Ⓓ
13	1400 Walters Ave.	A	B	C	D	Ⓐ Ⓑ Ⓒ Ⓓ
14	200 N. 32nd Street	A	B	C	D	Ⓐ Ⓑ Ⓒ Ⓓ

	Delivery Address	Delivery Route				Answer Grid
15	110 Walters Ave.	A	B	C	D	Ⓐ Ⓑ Ⓒ Ⓓ
16	1100 Elton Parkway	A	B	C	D	Ⓐ Ⓑ Ⓒ Ⓓ
17	1500 Veronica Ave.	A	B	C	D	Ⓐ Ⓑ Ⓒ Ⓓ
18	850 Elton Parkway	A	B	C	D	Ⓐ Ⓑ Ⓒ Ⓓ
19	500 Victory Blvd.	A	B	C	D	Ⓐ Ⓑ Ⓒ Ⓓ
20	55 N. 32nd Street	A	B	C	D	Ⓐ Ⓑ Ⓒ Ⓓ
21	897 Wilmington Drive	A	B	C	D	Ⓐ Ⓑ Ⓒ Ⓓ
22	400 Decatur Ave.	A	B	C	D	Ⓐ Ⓑ Ⓒ Ⓓ
23	300 N. 32nd Street	A	B	C	D	Ⓐ Ⓑ Ⓒ Ⓓ
24	1201 Walters Ave.	A	B	C	D	Ⓐ Ⓑ Ⓒ Ⓓ
25	200 Walters Ave.	A	B	C	D	Ⓐ Ⓑ Ⓒ Ⓓ
26	908 Fillmore Ave.	A	B	C	D	Ⓐ Ⓑ Ⓒ Ⓓ
27	1500 Elton Parkway	A	B	C	D	Ⓐ Ⓑ Ⓒ Ⓓ
28	1300 Walters Ave.	A	B	C	D	Ⓐ Ⓑ Ⓒ Ⓓ
29	2500 Veronica Ave.	A	B	C	D	Ⓐ Ⓑ Ⓒ Ⓓ
30	900 Victory Blvd.	A	B	C	D	Ⓐ Ⓑ Ⓒ Ⓓ
31	150 N. 32nd Street	A	B	C	D	Ⓐ Ⓑ Ⓒ Ⓓ
32	2500 Walters Ave.	A	B	C	D	Ⓐ Ⓑ Ⓒ Ⓓ
33	250 N. 32nd Street	A	B	C	D	Ⓐ Ⓑ Ⓒ Ⓓ
34	4000 Veronica Ave.	A	B	C	D	Ⓐ Ⓑ Ⓒ Ⓓ
35	1800 Elton Parkway	A	B	C	D	Ⓐ Ⓑ Ⓒ Ⓓ
36	745 Elton Parkway	A	B	C	D	Ⓐ Ⓑ Ⓒ Ⓓ

Memory Practice Test #1:   Coding Guide

Range of Addresses	Delivery Route
You have 5 minutes to memorize the Coding Guide on page 78, then code the following 36 addresses based on your <u>memory</u> of the coding guide. **(On the actual test you will probably have several minutes to practice answering coding questions. Those minutes can also be used, if you wish, to further memorize the codes.)** **You have 7 minutes to answer the following 36 coding questions.**	

	Delivery Address	Delivery Route				Answer Grid
1	200 Elton Parkway	A	B	C	D	Ⓐ Ⓑ Ⓒ Ⓓ
2	190 N. 32nd Street	A	B	C	D	Ⓐ Ⓑ Ⓒ Ⓓ
3	150 Walters Ave.	A	B	C	D	Ⓐ Ⓑ Ⓒ Ⓓ
4	600 Veronica Ave.	A	B	C	D	Ⓐ Ⓑ Ⓒ Ⓓ
5	1100 Elton Parkway	A	B	C	D	Ⓐ Ⓑ Ⓒ Ⓓ
6	50 N. 32nd Street	A	B	C	D	Ⓐ Ⓑ Ⓒ Ⓓ
7	210 Walters Ave.	A	B	C	D	Ⓐ Ⓑ Ⓒ Ⓓ
8	900 Walker Ave.	A	B	C	D	Ⓐ Ⓑ Ⓒ Ⓓ
9	175 Walters Ave.	A	B	C	D	Ⓐ Ⓑ Ⓒ Ⓓ
10	7000 Veronica Ave.	A	B	C	D	Ⓐ Ⓑ Ⓒ Ⓓ
11	2000 Elton Parkway	A	B	C	D	Ⓐ Ⓑ Ⓒ Ⓓ
12	150 N. 32nd Street	A	B	C	D	Ⓐ Ⓑ Ⓒ Ⓓ
13	900 Elton Parkway	A	B	C	D	Ⓐ Ⓑ Ⓒ Ⓓ
14	1900 Victory Blvd.	A	B	C	D	Ⓐ Ⓑ Ⓒ Ⓓ

	Delivery Address	Delivery Route				Answer Grid
15	100 Victory Blvd.	A	B	C	D	Ⓐ Ⓑ Ⓒ Ⓓ
16	75 Delmar Street	A	B	C	D	Ⓐ Ⓑ Ⓒ Ⓓ
17	400 Elton Parkway	A	B	C	D	Ⓐ Ⓑ Ⓒ Ⓓ
18	2175 Marville Ave.	A	B	C	D	Ⓐ Ⓑ Ⓒ Ⓓ
19	450 N. 32nd Street	A	B	C	D	Ⓐ Ⓑ Ⓒ Ⓓ
20	1201 Walters Ave.	A	B	C	D	Ⓐ Ⓑ Ⓒ Ⓓ
21	200 Walters Ave.	A	B	C	D	Ⓐ Ⓑ Ⓒ Ⓓ
22	900 Victory Blvd.	A	B	C	D	Ⓐ Ⓑ Ⓒ Ⓓ
23	120 N. 32nd Street	A	B	C	D	Ⓐ Ⓑ Ⓒ Ⓓ
24	375 Bakers Ave.	A	B	C	D	Ⓐ Ⓑ Ⓒ Ⓓ
25	900 Veronica Ave.	A	B	C	D	Ⓐ Ⓑ Ⓒ Ⓓ
26	200 Farmers Ave.	A	B	C	D	Ⓐ Ⓑ Ⓒ Ⓓ
27	1500 Elton Parkway	A	B	C	D	Ⓐ Ⓑ Ⓒ Ⓓ
28	125 Victory Blvd.	A	B	C	D	Ⓐ Ⓑ Ⓒ Ⓓ
29	2500 Walters Ave.	A	B	C	D	Ⓐ Ⓑ Ⓒ Ⓓ
30	5000 Veronica Ave.	A	B	C	D	Ⓐ Ⓑ Ⓒ Ⓓ
31	190 Walters Ave.	A	B	C	D	Ⓐ Ⓑ Ⓒ Ⓓ
32	290 N. 32nd Street	A	B	C	D	Ⓐ Ⓑ Ⓒ Ⓓ
33	1500 Walters Ave.	A	B	C	D	Ⓐ Ⓑ Ⓒ Ⓓ
34	840 Furman Street	A	B	C	D	Ⓐ Ⓑ Ⓒ Ⓓ
35	550 Elton Parkway	A	B	C	D	Ⓐ Ⓑ Ⓒ Ⓓ
36	225 N. 32nd Street	A	B	C	D	Ⓐ Ⓑ Ⓒ Ⓓ

Answers: Practice Test #1

Address Checking

1. B	7. A	13. C	19. D	25. D	31. D	37. C	43. D	49. B	55. C
2. A	8. C	14. A	20. A	26. A	32. B	38. D	44. D	50. D	56. D
3. D	9. D	15. B	21. C	27. B	33. A	39. C	45. A	51. B	57. B
4. A	10. A	16. D	22. B	28. D	34. D	40. A	46. C	52. C	58. C
5. B	11. B	17. B	23. A	29. A	35. B	41. D	47. D	53. B	59. A
6. A	12. C	18. A	24. C	30. B	36. A	42. C	48. C	54. C	60. B

Forms Completion

1. D	6. D	11. B	16. C	21. D	26. B
2. C	7. D	12. A	17. B	22. B	27. C
3. B	8. C	13. C	18. B	23. C	28. D
4. C	9. A	14. D	19. C	24. B	29. C
5. C	10. D	15. B	20. D	25. D	30. C

Coding

1. B	5. B	9. A	13. C	17. C	21. D	25. A	29. C	33. B
2. A	6. C	10. D	14. B	18. A	22. D	26. D	30. C	34. C
3. C	7. A	11. A	15. A	19. C	23. B	27. B	31. A	35. B
4. A	8. C	12. D	16. B	20. A	24. C	28. C	32. D	36. A

Memory

1. A	5. B	9. A	13. A	17. A	21. A	25. C	29. D	33. C
2. B	6. A	10. D	14. D	18. D	22. C	26. D	30. C	34. D
3. A	7. C	11. B	15. C	19. D	23. A	27. B	31. A	35. A
4. C	8. D	12. A	16. D	20. C	24. D	28. C	32. B	36. B

PRACTICE TEST

Part	Time Allowed	Number of Ques.	Description of Question
1. Address Checking	11 minutes	60	**Compare two addresses.**
2. Forms Completion	15 minutes	30	Correctly complete forms.
3. Coding	6 minutes	36	Find correct code for an address.
4. Memory (of coding examples, above)	7 minutes	36	Memorize address codes (which are same as codes in the "Coding" section part of the test.)

The first Part of this practice test is ADDRESS CHECKING.

(You have 11 minutes to complete this part of the test.)

When you are ready, turn the page and start the test.

Address Checking Practice Test 2: Below are 60 pairs of addresses. You have 11 minutes to compare each pair for errors and mark the answer sheet to indicate errors found as follows:

A. No Errors   **B.** Address Only   **C.** Zip Code Only   **D.** Both Address and ZIP Code

	Correct List of Addresses		Address List to be Checked		
	Address	**ZIP**	**Address**	**ZIP**	**Answer Grid**
1	650 Boulder Ave. Yuma, MN	30467	620 Boulder Ave. Yuma, MN	30467	A B C D
2	1040 Narrow Rd. Williams, MS	09391	1040 Narrow Rd. Williams, MS	00391	A B C D
3	P.O. Box 6062 Payson, SC	02018-3798	P.O. Box 6065 Payson, SC	02018-3793	A B C D
4	4238 Felder Way Glendale, AK	10912	4238 Felder Way Glendale, AK	10912	A B C D
5	563 Trader Ave. Miami, TX	42803-3425	563 Trader Ave. Miami, TX	42803-3455	A B C D
6	2671 JFK Pkwy. Willis, NY	06693-1012	2671 JFK Pkwy. Willis, NY	06693-1012	A B C D
7	3542 Carren St. Sedonia, MI	11004-2779	3542 Careen St. Sedonia, MI	11004-2719	A B C D
8	196 Venen Ct. Mesa, MA	98813	196 Venen Ave. Mesa, MA	98813	A B C D
9	663 Delva Street Florence, AR	12412-4343	663 Delva Street Florence, AR	12412-4343	A B C D
10	900 Reyes St. Chandler, CA	54001	90 Reyes St. Chandler, CA	24001	A B C D
11	4224 York Road Sierra, OR	03662-4891	4225 York Road Sierra, OR	03662-4891	A B C D
12	562 Trader Ave. Somerton, CT	52729	562 Trader Ave. Somerton, CT	55729	A B C D
13	6084 Overton Ln. Peoria, OH	47901-4189	608 Overton Ln. Peoria, OH	47901-4139	A B C D
14	9372 Island Cir. Eloy, IL	87499-4679	9372 Island Cir. Eloy, IL	87499-4676	A B C D
15	2876 Elderts Ln. Jamaica, NY	11302	2376 Elderts Ln. Jamaica, NY	11302	A B C D

Address Checking Practice Test 2 (cont'd):

Address Checking Practice Test 2 (cont'd): Continue to compare each pair of addresses for errors and mark the answer sheet as follows:

A. No Errors　　**B.** Address Only　　**C.** Zip Code Only　　**D.** Both Address and ZIP Code

	Correct List of Addresses		**Address List to be Checked**		
	Address	**ZIP**	**Address**	**ZIP**	**Answer Grid**
16	4325 Ludder Rd. Walton, MS	70467	4325 Ludder Rd. Walton, MA	70467	A B C D
17	3254 Barnes St. Willerd, MS	03391	3254 Barn St. Willerd, MS	03891	A B C D
18	P.O. Box 4039 Quiet, NY	02028-3743	P.O. Box 4039 Quiet, NY	02028-3743	A B C D
19	7738 Field Way Ferndale, CA	90412	738 Field Way Ferndale, CA	90412	A B C D
20	8634 Tungs Ave. Atlas, TX	52603-7422	8684 Tungs Ave. Atlas, TX	52603-7425	A B C D
21	6671 Acer Pkwy. James, FL	04653-5392	6671 Acer Pkwy. James, FL	04653-5392	A B C D
22	4542 Karns St. Seldon, MI	31044-3713	4542 Karns St. Seldon, MI	31044-3718	A B C D
23	7963 Mirage Ct. Lima, MA	57893	796 Mirage Ct. Lima, MA	57863	A B C D
24	2632 Herker St. Rome, MN	32413-2347	2632 Herken St. Rome, MN	32413-2347	A B C D
25	5990 Marina St. Charmer, CA	84401	5990 Marina St. Charmer, CA	84401	A B C D
26	2254 Jersey Road Niece, OR	33429-4921	2254 Jersey Road Neice, OR	33429-4921	A B C D
27	8375 Turk Ave. Sonya, NJ	22325	8375 Turk Ave. Sonya, NJ	22322	A B C D
28	1039 Linker Ln. Newton, IL	47267	1039 Linker Ln. Newton, IL	47267	A B C D
29	1599 Somer Lane Perry, WA	87207-3189	1599 Sumer Lane Perry, WA	87201-3189	A B C D
30	7292 Island Cir. Danker, SC	87684	7292 Island Cir. Danker, SC	87634	A B C D

Address Checking Practice Test 2 (cont'd): Continue to compare each pair of addresses for errors and mark the answer sheet as follows:

A. No Errors   **B.** Address Only   **C.** Zip Code Only   **D.** Both Address and ZIP Code

	Correct List of Addresses		Address List to be Checked		
	Address	**ZIP**	**Address**	**ZIP**	**Answer Grid**
31	3325 Lumer Rd. Felton, FL	27662-5256	325 Lumer Rd. Felton, FL	27662-5256	Ⓐ Ⓑ Ⓒ Ⓓ
32	527 Comfort Ln. Tempe, WA	27840	527 Cumfort Ln. Tempe, WA	27340	Ⓐ Ⓑ Ⓒ Ⓓ
33	4413 Rama Ave. Taylor, MO	22920-8319	4413 Ramu Ave. Taylor, MO	22920-8319	Ⓐ Ⓑ Ⓒ Ⓓ
34	109 Binion Street Prescott, RI	54462	109 Binion Street Prescott, RI	24462	Ⓐ Ⓑ Ⓒ Ⓓ
35	1537 Venian Ct. Fredonia, FL	11301-6166	1537 Venian Ct. Fredonia, FL	11301-6166	Ⓐ Ⓑ Ⓒ Ⓓ
36	P.O. Box 4012 Gilbert, MS	78454	P.O. Box 4012 Gilbert, MD	78424	Ⓐ Ⓑ Ⓒ Ⓓ
37	291 Ventura Ter. Stafford, AK	35912	291 Ventura Ter. Stafford, AR	35912	Ⓐ Ⓑ Ⓒ Ⓓ
38	5784 Manor Way San Luis, MD	72298-2120	5784 Manor Way San Leo, MD	72298-2120	Ⓐ Ⓑ Ⓒ Ⓓ
39	3739 Spring St. Hayden, NJ	43550	3739 Spring St. Hayden, NJ	43500	Ⓐ Ⓑ Ⓒ Ⓓ
40	854 Center Ave. Clark, VA	33483-0108	854 Center Ave. Clark, VA	33483-1008	Ⓐ Ⓑ Ⓒ Ⓓ
41	672 Bahama Cir. Avon, ME	82601-8273	672 Bahama Cir. Avon, ME	82601-8273	Ⓐ Ⓑ Ⓒ Ⓓ
42	4153 Clay Ave. Parker, KS	40451-7214	453 Clay Ave. Parker, KS	40451-7514	Ⓐ Ⓑ Ⓒ Ⓓ
43	737 Grand Lane Marana, PA	75684	737 Grand Lane Marana, PA	75684	Ⓐ Ⓑ Ⓒ Ⓓ
44	1591 Custard St. Hudson, IL	38564	1591 Custerd St. Hudson, IL	38564	Ⓐ Ⓑ Ⓒ Ⓓ
45	1618 Huron Rd. Duncan, NJ	20127-4341	1618 Horon Rd. Duncan, NJ	20157-4341	Ⓐ Ⓑ Ⓒ Ⓓ

Address Checking Practice Test 2 (cont'd): Continue to compare each pair of addresses for errors and mark the answer sheet as follows:

A. No Errors   **B.** Address Only   **C.** Zip Code Only   **D.** Both Address and ZIP Code

	Correct List of Addresses		Address List to be Checked		
	Address	ZIP	Address	ZIP	Answer Grid
46	4617 Indy Ln. Warren, AR	07016-4361	4617 Indy Ln. Warren, AR	07016-4367	A B C D
47	2729 Over Ave. Tucker, NY	47603	2729 Over Ave. Tucker, NY	47603	A B C D
48	3415 Bonner Rd. Rector, OH	35029	3415 Boner Rd. Rector, OH	35029	A B C D
49	9624 Gator Way Wynne, OR	01702-4177	9624 Gator Way Wynne, OR	01702-4117	A B C D
50	6617 Coral Lane Prescott, AK	07214	667 Coral Lane Prescott, AK	07224	A B C D
51	5779 China Pkwy. Branch, NJ	84203-3254	579 China Pkwy. Branch, NJ	84208-3254	A B C D
52	1167 Wells Ct. Viola, MD	60396-1009	167 Wells Ct. Viola, MD	60396-1009	A B C D
53	1244 Slattery St. Marshall, FL	12010-1297	1244 Slattery St. Marshall, FL	12010-1297	A B C D
54	2439 Harbor St. Conway, VA	89313	2439 Harbor St. Conway, VA	89318	A B C D
55	3429 Shop Ave. Jersey, PA	11242-4433	349 Shop Ave. Jersey, PA	11242-4433	A B C D
56	5705 Ash St. Buffalo, KS	24001	5705 Ash St. Buffalo, KS	54001	A B C D
57	2112 Dawn Cir. Marion, MS	23602-7151	2112 Dawn Cir. Marion, MS	23602-7151	A B C D
58	6794 Center St. Eudora, RI	57922	674 Center St. Eudora, RI	57923	A B C D
59	P.O. Box 0712 Gentry, WA	62976	P.O. Box 0712 Gentry, WA	62979	A B C D
60	1719 East Rd. Wright, MO	90147-3194	1719 East Rd. Wright, MO	90147-3194	A B C D

Forms Completion Practice Test 2

This part of the test consists of 5 different forms and 30 questions relating to the 5 forms. Study each form and then answer the questions following each of the forms.

(Time allowed: 15 minutes for 30 questions).

Answer questions 1 – 6 based on the following form:

STATEMENT FOR PICKUP SERVICE		
1. Information (Product)		**2. Information (Customer)**
Type of pickup service	**Quantity**	13. First and Last Name
3. Priority Mail	8.	14. Company Name
4. Express Mail	9.	15. Address 1.
5. Parcel Post	10.	16. Address 2
6.Global Express Guaranteed	11.	17. City
		18. State.
7. Estimated weight (total) of all packages (in pounds)	12.	19. Zip + 4
20. Affix stamps or Meter Strip in this space		**Method of Payment**
		21. □ Metered Postage or Stamps
		22. □ Postage Due Account
		23. □ Express Mail Corporate Account Number
		24. □ Check (Payable to Postmaster)
		25. □ Label For Merchandise Return
26. Signature of Customer	27. Signature of USPS employee	28. Pickup Date and Time

	Question	Answer Grid
1	In which box would you indicate that the mail articles were picked up on September 12, 2010? A. 20　　　B. 26　　　C. 28　　　D. 2	Ⓐ Ⓑ Ⓒ Ⓓ
2	The stamps should be affixed in box: A. 8　　　B. 20　　　C. 5　　　D. 8	Ⓐ Ⓑ Ⓒ Ⓓ
3	Where on this form should the postal employee sign? A. 26　　　B. 27　　　C. 13　　　D. 28	Ⓐ Ⓑ Ⓒ Ⓓ
4	Which of the following is a correct entry for box 10? A. Express　　　B. 9/10/10　　　C. $4.50　　　D. 8	Ⓐ Ⓑ Ⓒ Ⓓ
5	The customer paid $13.00 in the form of stamps. Which box should be checked? A. 21　　　B. 7　　　C. 24　　　D. 22	Ⓐ Ⓑ Ⓒ Ⓓ
6	The customer's Zip+4 number is 11201-3765. This should be indicated in box: A. 19　　　B. 9　　　C. 10　　　D. 20	Ⓐ Ⓑ Ⓒ Ⓓ

(Answers for Test 2 are on page 102.)

Answer questions 7 – 12 based on the following form:

RECEIPT FOR REGISTERED MAIL			
1.This section is to be completed by the post office.	2.Registered Number:	4. Date Stamp	
	3. Registration Fee $ _____	5. Charge for Handling	8. Fee for Return Receipt
		6. Postage Amount	9. Fee for Restricted Delivery
		7. Received by	
10. This section is to be completed by the postal customer. Please PRINT with ballpoint pen, or TYPE.	11. TO:		
	12. FROM:		
FORM # 7477 (Copy 1 – Customer) (Copy 2 – Post Office) (See information on reverse side of this form.)			

	Question	Answer Grid
7	The Registration Fee is $9.75 and the Postage Amount is $2.85. What amount should be entered in box 6? A. 12.60 　　　 B. 2.85 　　　 C. 9.75 　　　 D. 12	Ⓐ Ⓑ Ⓒ Ⓓ
8	The address where the mail is being sent to should be entered in box: A. 11 　　　 B. 12 　　　 C. 7 　　　 D. 4	Ⓐ Ⓑ Ⓒ Ⓓ
9	The customer wishes Restricted Delivery. In which box should the fee for restricted delivery be entered? A. 5 　　　 B. 6 　　　 C. 8 　　　 D. 9	Ⓐ Ⓑ Ⓒ Ⓓ
10	Which of the following boxes should be completed by the postal customer? A. 7 　　　 B. 9 　　　 C. 3 　　　 D. 11	Ⓐ Ⓑ Ⓒ Ⓓ
11	The name of the postal employee who processes the Receipt For Registered Mail should be entered in which box? A. 11 　　　 B. 12 　　　 C. 1 　　　 D. 7	Ⓐ Ⓑ Ⓒ Ⓓ
12	The date stamp should be stamped in box: A. 1 　　　 B. 2 　　　 C. 3 　　　 D. 4	Ⓐ Ⓑ Ⓒ Ⓓ

(Answers for Test 2 are on page 102.)

Answer questions 13 – 18 based on the following form:

1. RECEIPT FOR INSURED MAIL		
15.	2. Postage	6. ☐ Fragile 7. ☐ Perishable
		8. ☐ Liquid 9. ☐ Hazardous
	3. Insurance Fee	10.
		11. Stamp Postmark Here
	4. Handling Fee	
	5. Total (Postage plus Fees) $_____	
12. Addressee (Sent to):		
13. Street, Apt. Number; or PO Box Number		
14. City, State and ZIP		

	Question	Answer Grid
13	The first and last name of the person to whom the mail is being sent should be entered in box: A. 14 B. 13 C. 9 D. 12	Ⓐ Ⓑ Ⓒ Ⓓ
14	The postmark should be stamped in box: A. 8 B. 9 C. 5 D. 11	Ⓐ Ⓑ Ⓒ Ⓓ
15	The ZIP code of the addressee must be entered in box: A. 12 B. 13 C. 14 D. 15	Ⓐ Ⓑ Ⓒ Ⓓ
16	In which of the following boxes is a "check mark" appropriate? A. 6 B. 15 C. 2 D. 10	Ⓐ Ⓑ Ⓒ Ⓓ
17	Postage is $2.00. Handling Fee is $4.50. Insurance Fee is $3.25. What is the correct amount to be entered in box 5? A. 8.75: B. 9.75 C. 7.75 D. 9.00	Ⓐ Ⓑ Ⓒ Ⓓ
18	The PO Box Number of the addressee must be entered in which box? A. 14 B. 13 C. 10 D. 11	Ⓐ Ⓑ Ⓒ Ⓓ

(Answers for Test 2 are on page 102.)

Answer questions 19 – 24 based on the following form:

Application for Nonprofit Standard Mail Prices	
1. Legal Name of Organization	2. Street Address (including Street/Suite Number)
	3. City, State, Zip
4. Telephone	5. E-mail address
6. Alternate mailing address (if any)	
Type of Organization (Check only one box) 7. ☐ Educational 8. ☐ Religious 9. ☐ Scientific 10. ☐ Labor 11. ☐ Veterans	
12. Has this organization previously mailed at nonprofit standard prices? 13. ☐ YES 14. ☐ NO	15. If the answer to 12 is "YES", have standard mail privileges ever been revoked? 16. ☐ YES 17. ☐ NO
18. Signature of applicant	19. Title of applicant
20. Date this request is submitted.	21.

	Question	Answer Grid
19	In which box should the name of the organization be entered? A. 1　　　　　B. 2　　　　　C. 3　　　　　D. 21	Ⓐ Ⓑ Ⓒ Ⓓ
20	The organization is a non-profit Labor organization. Based on this, box ___ should be checked. A. 8　　　　　B. 9　　　　　C. 5　　　　　D. 10	Ⓐ Ⓑ Ⓒ Ⓓ
21	Where on this form should the applicant sign? A. 18　　　　　B. 20　　　　　C. 1　　　　　D. 3	Ⓐ Ⓑ Ⓒ Ⓓ
22	Which of the following is a correct entry for box 4? A. 11214B　　B. 718-674-2456　C. 1/10　　　D. 16	Ⓐ Ⓑ Ⓒ Ⓓ
23	The customer previously mailed at nonprofit standard prices. Based on this, which box should be checked? A. 12　　　　　B. 13　　　　　C. 14　　　　　D. 21	Ⓐ Ⓑ Ⓒ Ⓓ
24	The Application for Nonprofit Standard Mail Prices was submitted on July 7, 2010. This date should be entered in which box? A. 1　　　　　B. 18　　　　　C. 21　　　　　D. 20	Ⓐ Ⓑ Ⓒ Ⓓ

(Answers for Test 2 are on page 102.)

Answer questions 25 – 30 based on the following form:

CLAIM FOR DOMESTIC OR INTERNATIONAL MAIL					
2. Addressee Information			**3. Mailer Information**		
4. Last Name	5.MI	6. First Name	7. Last Name	8.MI	9. First Name
10. Business Name (if addressee is a company)			11. Business Name (if mailer is a company)		
12. Address (Number and Street)			13. Address (Number and Street)		
14. Address (Suite or Apartment Number)			15. Address (Suite or Apartment Number)		
16. City State Zip			17. City State Zip		
18. E-mail Address (Optional)			19. E-mail Address (Optional)		

20. Description of Missing Lost or Damaged Contents				
21. Item codes: 01 Jewelry, 02 Electronics, 03 Computers, 04 Animals, 05 Firearms, 06 Event Tickets, 07 Sports Equipment, 08 Collectibles, 09 Clothing, 10 Cash, 11 Other.				
22. Describe the contents and check off (L) for Lost or (D) for damaged				
23. Item	24. Description of contents	25.(L)or(D)	26.Item code	27.Value or Repair Cost in $
1		L □ D □		
2		L □ D □		
3		L □ D □		
		28. Total Value or Repair Cost in $		
29. The customer submitting the claim is the □ Mailer □ Addressee				
30. Payment is to be made to the □ Mailer □ Addressee				
31. Signature of Postal Customer submitting Claim		32. Date signed (MM/DD/YYYY)		

	Question	Answer Grid
25	The first name of the customer who mailed the article should be entered in which box? A. 6　　　　B. 4　　　　C. 7　　　　D. 9	Ⓐ Ⓑ Ⓒ Ⓓ
26	The e-mail address of the Addressee should be entered in which box? A. 18　　　B. 19　　　C. 12　　　D. 13	Ⓐ Ⓑ Ⓒ Ⓓ
27	In which box on this form should the customer submitting the claim sign? A. 32　　　B. 31　　　C. 4　　　D. 7	Ⓐ Ⓑ Ⓒ Ⓓ
28	The missing item is a computer. The item code is therefore: A. 21　　　B. 01　　　C. 02　　　D. 03	Ⓐ Ⓑ Ⓒ Ⓓ
29	Which of the following is a correct entry for box 32? A. May 21, 2010　B. 7/21/10　　C. 10/20/2010　　D. 1/9	Ⓐ Ⓑ Ⓒ Ⓓ
30	The middle initial of the Mailer should be entered in which box? A. 5　　　　B. 8　　　　C. 4　　　　D. 7	Ⓐ Ⓑ Ⓒ Ⓓ

Directions for the following 36 Coding Questions

For each of the following 36 "Delivery Addresses" determine based on the coding guide whether the address belongs to Delivery Route A, B, C or D, and mark your answer grid accordingly. You have 6 minutes to code the 36 addresses.

Coding Practice Test # 2:   Coding Guide

Range of Addresses	Delivery Route
50 – 400 S. 9th Street 10 – 99 Jackson Lane 10 – 200 Willis Ave.	A
100 – 500 Jackson Lane 401 – 1000 S. 9th Street	B
2000 – 8000 Dover Place 1 – 100 Emperor Drive 201 – 2500 Willis Ave.	C
All mail that doesn't fall in one of the address ranges listed above	D

	Delivery Address	Delivery Route				Answer Grid
1	10 Willis Ave.	A	B	C	D	Ⓐ Ⓑ Ⓒ Ⓓ
2	105 Jackson Lane	A	B	C	D	Ⓐ Ⓑ Ⓒ Ⓓ
3	2000 Dover Place	A	B	C	D	Ⓐ Ⓑ Ⓒ Ⓓ
4	420 S. 9th Street	A	B	C	D	Ⓐ Ⓑ Ⓒ Ⓓ
5	300 Willis Ave.	A	B	C	D	Ⓐ Ⓑ Ⓒ Ⓓ
6	80 S. 9th Street	A	B	C	D	Ⓐ Ⓑ Ⓒ Ⓓ
7	350 Jackson Lane	A	B	C	D	Ⓐ Ⓑ Ⓒ Ⓓ
8	10 Jackson Lane	A	B	C	D	Ⓐ Ⓑ Ⓒ Ⓓ
9	9000 Dover Place	A	B	C	D	Ⓐ Ⓑ Ⓒ Ⓓ
10	200 Willis Ave.	A	B	C	D	Ⓐ Ⓑ Ⓒ Ⓓ
11	6000 Dover Place	A	B	C	D	Ⓐ Ⓑ Ⓒ Ⓓ
12	250 S. 9th Street	A	B	C	D	Ⓐ Ⓑ Ⓒ Ⓓ
13	10 Emperor Drive	A	B	C	D	Ⓐ Ⓑ Ⓒ Ⓓ
14	89 Jackson Lane	A	B	C	D	Ⓐ Ⓑ Ⓒ Ⓓ

	Delivery Address	Delivery Route				Answer Grid
15	501 S. 9th Street	A	B	C	D	(A) (B) (C) (D)
16	379 Jackson Lane	A	B	C	D	(A) (B) (C) (D)
17	649 Prospect Park	A	B	C	D	(A) (B) (C) (D)
18	350 S. 9th Street	A	B	C	D	(A) (B) (C) (D)
19	7650 Dover Place	A	B	C	D	(A) (B) (C) (D)
20	620 Willis Ave.	A	B	C	D	(A) (B) (C) (D)
21	867 S. 9th Street	A	B	C	D	(A) (B) (C) (D)
22	2800 Dinkens Ave.	A	B	C	D	(A) (B) (C) (D)
23	375 S. 9th Street	A	B	C	D	(A) (B) (C) (D)
24	8100 Dover Place	A	B	C	D	(A) (B) (C) (D)
25	75 Emperor Drive	A	B	C	D	(A) (B) (C) (D)
26	100 Willis Ave.	A	B	C	D	(A) (B) (C) (D)
27	770 S. 9th Street	A	B	C	D	(A) (B) (C) (D)
28	100 Emperor Drive	A	B	C	D	(A) (B) (C) (D)
29	2400 Willis Ave.	A	B	C	D	(A) (B) (C) (D)
30	99 Jackson Lane	A	B	C	D	(A) (B) (C) (D)
31	145 Willis Ave.	A	B	C	D	(A) (B) (C) (D)
32	90 Emperor Drive	A	B	C	D	(A) (B) (C) (D)
33	55 Jackson Lane	A	B	C	D	(A) (B) (C) (D)
34	470 Jackson Lane	A	B	C	D	(A) (B) (C) (D)
35	490 Fennimore Lane	A	B	C	D	(A) (B) (C) (D)
36	6500 Dover Place	A	B	C	D	(A) (B) (C) (D)

Memory Practice Test #2:   Coding Guide

Range of Addresses	Delivery Route

You have 5 minutes to memorize the Coding Guide on page 98, then code the following 36 addresses based on your <u>memory</u> of the coding guide.

(On the actual test you will probably have several minutes to practice answering coding questions. Those minutes can also be used, if you wish, to further memorize the codes.)

You have 7 minutes to answer the following 36 coding questions.

	Delivery Address	Delivery Route				Answer Grid
1	50 Jackson Lane	A	B	C	D	Ⓐ Ⓑ Ⓒ Ⓓ
2	2000 Dover Place	A	B	C	D	Ⓐ Ⓑ Ⓒ Ⓓ
3	200 Willis Ave.	A	B	C	D	Ⓐ Ⓑ Ⓒ Ⓓ
4	890 Blanding Road	A	B	C	D	Ⓐ Ⓑ Ⓒ Ⓓ
5	400 Jackson Lane	A	B	C	D	Ⓐ Ⓑ Ⓒ Ⓓ
6	90 Jackson Lane	A	B	C	D	Ⓐ Ⓑ Ⓒ Ⓓ
7	3500 Willis Ave.	A	B	C	D	Ⓐ Ⓑ Ⓒ Ⓓ
8	444 S. 9th Street	A	B	C	D	Ⓐ Ⓑ Ⓒ Ⓓ
9	2800 Charles Drive	A	B	C	D	Ⓐ Ⓑ Ⓒ Ⓓ
10	210 Willis Ave.	A	B	C	D	Ⓐ Ⓑ Ⓒ Ⓓ
11	50 S. 9th Street	A	B	C	D	Ⓐ Ⓑ Ⓒ Ⓓ
12	10 Emperor Drive	A	B	C	D	Ⓐ Ⓑ Ⓒ Ⓓ
13	190 Jackson Lane	A	B	C	D	Ⓐ Ⓑ Ⓒ Ⓓ
14	100 Willis Ave.	A	B	C	D	Ⓐ Ⓑ Ⓒ Ⓓ

	Delivery Address	Delivery Route				Answer Grid
15	6000 Dover Place	A	B	C	D	Ⓐ Ⓑ Ⓒ Ⓓ
16	410 Jackson Lane	A	B	C	D	Ⓐ Ⓑ Ⓒ Ⓓ
17	350 S. 9th Street	A	B	C	D	Ⓐ Ⓑ Ⓒ Ⓓ
18	777 S. 9th Street	A	B	C	D	Ⓐ Ⓑ Ⓒ Ⓓ
19	200 Emperor Drive	A	B	C	D	Ⓐ Ⓑ Ⓒ Ⓓ
20	150 Willis Ave.	A	B	C	D	Ⓐ Ⓑ Ⓒ Ⓓ
21	2500 Willis Ave.	A	B	C	D	Ⓐ Ⓑ Ⓒ Ⓓ
22	865 S. 9th Street	A	B	C	D	Ⓐ Ⓑ Ⓒ Ⓓ
23	100 Elmers Lane	A	B	C	D	Ⓐ Ⓑ Ⓒ Ⓓ
24	200 S. 9th Street	A	B	C	D	Ⓐ Ⓑ Ⓒ Ⓓ
25	120 Willis Ave.	A	B	C	D	Ⓐ Ⓑ Ⓒ Ⓓ
26	90 Emperor Drive	A	B	C	D	Ⓐ Ⓑ Ⓒ Ⓓ
27	60 Jackson Lane	A	B	C	D	Ⓐ Ⓑ Ⓒ Ⓓ
28	7000 Dover Place	A	B	C	D	Ⓐ Ⓑ Ⓒ Ⓓ
29	436 Jackson Lane	A	B	C	D	Ⓐ Ⓑ Ⓒ Ⓓ
30	50 Emperor Drive	A	B	C	D	Ⓐ Ⓑ Ⓒ Ⓓ
31	280 S. 9th Street	A	B	C	D	Ⓐ Ⓑ Ⓒ Ⓓ
32	1000 Emperor Drive	A	B	C	D	Ⓐ Ⓑ Ⓒ Ⓓ
33	900 S. 9th Street	A	B	C	D	Ⓐ Ⓑ Ⓒ Ⓓ
34	820 Willis Ave.	A	B	C	D	Ⓐ Ⓑ Ⓒ Ⓓ
35	75 Jackson Lane	A	B	C	D	Ⓐ Ⓑ Ⓒ Ⓓ
36	5500 Dover Place	A	B	C	D	Ⓐ Ⓑ Ⓒ Ⓓ

Answers: Practice Test #2

Address Checking

1. B	7. D	13. D	19. B	25. A	31. B	37. B	43. A	49. C	55. B
2. C	8. B	14. C	20. D	26. B	32. D	38. B	44. B	50. D	56. C
3. D	9. A	15. B	21. A	27. C	33. B	39. C	45. D	51. D	57. A
4. A	10. D	16. B	22. C	28. A	34. C	40. C	46. C	52. B	58. D
5. C	11. B	17. D	23. D	29. D	35. A	41. A	47. A	53. A	59. C
6. A	12. C	18. A	24. B	30. C	36. D	42. D	48. B	54. C	60. A

Forms Completion

1. C	6. A	11. D	16. A	21. A	26. A
2. B	7. B	12. D	17. B	22. B	27. B
3. B	8. A	13. D	18. B	23. B	28. D
4. D	9. D	14. D	19. A	24. D	29. C
5. A	10. D	15. C	20. D	25. D	30. B

Coding

1. A	5. C	9. D	13. C	17. D	21. B	25. C	29. C	33. A
2. B	6. A	10. A	14. A	18. A	22. D	26. A	30. A	34. B
3. C	7. B	11. C	15. B	19. C	23. A	27. B	31. A	35. D
4. B	8. A	12. A	16. B	20. C	24. D	28. C	32. C	36. C

Memory

1. A	5. B	9. D	13. B	17. A	21. C	25. A	29. B	33. B
2. C	6. A	10. C	14. A	18. B	22. B	26. C	30. C	34. C
3. A	7. D	11. A	15. C	19. D	23. D	27. A	31. A	35. A
4. D	8. B	12. C	16. B	20. A	24. A	28. C	32. D	36. C

PRACTICE TEST

Part	Time Allowed	Number of Ques.	Description of Question
1. Address Checking	11 minutes	60	Compare two addresses.
2. Forms Completion	15 minutes	30	Correctly complete forms.
3. Coding	6 minutes	36	Find correct code for an address.
4. Memory (of coding examples, above)	7 minutes	36	Memorize address codes (which are same as codes in the "Coding" section part of the test.)

The first Part of this practice test is ADDRESS CHECKING.

(You have 11 minutes to complete this part of the test.)

When you are ready, turn the page and start the test.

———

Address Checking Practice Test 3: Below are 60 pairs of addresses. You have 11 minutes to compare each pair for errors and mark the answer sheet to indicate errors found as follows:

A. No Errors   **B.** Address Only   **C.** Zip Code Only   **D.** Both Address and ZIP Code

	Correct List of Addresses		Address List to be Checked		
	Address	**ZIP**	**Address**	**ZIP**	**Answer Grid**
1	4617 India Ln. Warren, AR	07016-4362	4617 India Ln. Watren, AR	07016-4362	Ⓐ Ⓑ Ⓒ Ⓓ
2	2729 Overly Ave. Tucker, NY	47603	2729 Overly Ave. Tucker, NJ	47603	Ⓐ Ⓑ Ⓒ Ⓓ
3	3415 Bonner Rd. Rector, OH	35029	3415 Bonner Rd. Rector, OH	35209	Ⓐ Ⓑ Ⓒ Ⓓ
4	9624 Kator Way Wynne, OR	01703-4717	9624 Gator Way Wynne, OR	01703-4117	Ⓐ Ⓑ Ⓒ Ⓓ
5	6617 Coral Lane Prescott, AK	07214	6617 Coral Lane Prescott, AK	07214	Ⓐ Ⓑ Ⓒ Ⓓ
6	779 China Pkwy. Brach, NJ	84203-8254	779 China Pkwy. Brach, NJ	84203-3254	Ⓐ Ⓑ Ⓒ Ⓓ
7	167 Welay Ct. Viola, MD	60396-1009	167 Velay Ct. Viola, MD	60396-1009	Ⓐ Ⓑ Ⓒ Ⓓ
8	1244 Slattery St. Marshall, FL	10201-1297	124 Slattery St. Marshall, FL	10201-7297	Ⓐ Ⓑ Ⓒ Ⓓ
9	439 Harbor Ave. Conway, VA	89318	439 Harbor Ave. Conway, VA	89318	Ⓐ Ⓑ Ⓒ Ⓓ
10	3377 Shop St. Jersey, PA	11245-4433	3377 Shop St. Jersey, PA	11242-4433	Ⓐ Ⓑ Ⓒ Ⓓ
11	5705 Ash Street Buffalo, KS	24001	5705 Ark Street Buffalo, KS	24001	Ⓐ Ⓑ Ⓒ Ⓓ
12	2112 Dawn Cir. Marion, MS	23605-7151	212 Dawn Cir. Marion, MS	23602-7151	Ⓐ Ⓑ Ⓒ Ⓓ
13	6794 Center St. Eudora, RI	57922	679 Center St. Eudora, RI	57922	Ⓐ Ⓑ Ⓒ Ⓓ
14	P.O. Box 0912 Bentry, WA	62979	P.O. Box 0912 Gentry, WA	62976	Ⓐ Ⓑ Ⓒ Ⓓ
15	171 Eastern Rd. Wright, MO	90147-3194	171 Eastern Rd. Wright, MO	90174-3194	Ⓐ Ⓑ Ⓒ Ⓓ

Address Checking Practice Test 3 (cont'd): Continue to compare each pair of addresses for errors and mark the answer sheet as follows:

A. No Errors   **B.** Address Only   **C.** Zip Code Only   **D.** Both Address and ZIP Code

	Correct List of Addresses		Address List to be Checked		
	Address	**ZIP**	**Address**	**ZIP**	**Answer Grid**
16	47 Kings Road Truman, PA	48779-4769	47 Kings Road Truman, PA	48779-4769	Ⓐ Ⓑ Ⓒ Ⓓ
17	2237 Tiger Street West Fork, SC	62627-5257	2237 Tiger Street East Fork, SC	62627-5257	Ⓐ Ⓑ Ⓒ Ⓓ
18	4326 Mirage Cir. Salem, KS	82047	4326 Mirage Cir. Salem, KS	82047	Ⓐ Ⓑ Ⓒ Ⓓ
19	5934 Paeder Ct. Rogers, CA	92328-8193	5934 Paeder Ct. Rogers, CA	92328-8193	Ⓐ Ⓑ Ⓒ Ⓓ
20	P.O. Box 3196 Stuggord, ME	55467	P.O. Box 3196 Stuggard, ME	55461	Ⓐ Ⓑ Ⓒ Ⓓ
21	7787 Capital St. Sidney, CT	31108-2772	7737 Capital St. Sidney, CT	31108-2772	Ⓐ Ⓑ Ⓒ Ⓓ
22	1482 Keller Way Atkins, TX	47482	1482 Keller Way Atkins, TX	47485	Ⓐ Ⓑ Ⓒ Ⓓ
23	630 Park Terrace Cabot, MI	92185	630 Park Terrace Cabot, MI	92135	Ⓐ Ⓑ Ⓒ Ⓓ
24	5534 Trump St. Newport, AR	27985-2419	5534 Trump St. Newport, AK	27982-2419	Ⓐ Ⓑ Ⓒ Ⓓ
25	3200 Faith Pkwy. Boles, NY	54035	3200 Faith Pkwy. Boles, NY	54035	Ⓐ Ⓑ Ⓒ Ⓓ
26	4394 Brock Ave. Gurdon, OR	43814-0702	4394 Brick Ave. Gurdon, OR	43814-0702	Ⓐ Ⓑ Ⓒ Ⓓ
27	632 Freedom Ln. Lowell, MA	68051-7281	6321 Freedom Ln. Lowell, MA	68051-7231	Ⓐ Ⓑ Ⓒ Ⓓ
28	527 Cactus Road Diaz, MN	14116-3293	527 Cactus Road Diaz, MN	14116-3293	Ⓐ Ⓑ Ⓒ Ⓓ
29	1698 Myers Cir. St. Joe, IL	28617	1693 Myers Cir. St. Joe, IL	28677	Ⓐ Ⓑ Ⓒ Ⓓ
30	2937 Justice Lane Stark City, MS	17490-9345	2937 Justice Lane Star City, MS	17490-9345	Ⓐ Ⓑ Ⓒ Ⓓ

Address Checking Practice Test 3 (cont'd): Continue to compare each pair of addresses for errors and mark the answer sheet as follows:

A. No Errors   **B.** Address Only   **C.** Zip Code Only   **D.** Both Address and ZIP Code

	Correct List of Addresses		Address List to be Checked		
	Address	**ZIP**	**Address**	**ZIP**	**Answer Grid**
31	9723 Jazon Lane Phoenix, KS	18221	9723 Jason Lane Phoenix, KS	18221	Ⓐ Ⓑ Ⓒ Ⓓ
32	72 Boulder Ct. Freemont, WA	39214-5245	72 Boulder Ct. Freemont, WA	39514-5245	Ⓐ Ⓑ Ⓒ Ⓓ
33	4653 Caserto St. Boise, ME	77104-1127	4653 Caserta St. Boise, ME	77104-1121	Ⓐ Ⓑ Ⓒ Ⓓ
34	583 Diamond St. Akron, MA	21175-8230	583 Damond St. Akron, MA	21115-8230	Ⓐ Ⓑ Ⓒ Ⓓ
35	3627 Hills Ave. Gilbert, CT	99024	3627 Hills Ave. Gilbert, CT	99024	Ⓐ Ⓑ Ⓒ Ⓓ
36	P.O. Box 7137 Garfand, NY	35223-4554	P.O. Box 7137 Garland, NY	35223-4554	Ⓐ Ⓑ Ⓒ Ⓓ
37	4388 Lewis Way Newark, SC	51812	4388 Lewis Way Newark, SC	51312	Ⓐ Ⓑ Ⓒ Ⓓ
38	747 Main Street Winston, MO	47303-9052	747 Main Street Winston, MO	47303-9052	Ⓐ Ⓑ Ⓒ Ⓓ
39	584 Fox Lane Stockton, IL	33630	5184 Fox Lane Stockton, IL	38630	Ⓐ Ⓑ Ⓒ Ⓓ
40	3116 Laker Road Jerome, TX	83701	3116 Laker Road Jerome, TX	83707	Ⓐ Ⓑ Ⓒ Ⓓ
41	612 Reasure Cir. Madison, MI	80152-2450	612 Reasure Cir. Madison, MI	80152-2450	Ⓐ Ⓑ Ⓒ Ⓓ
42	7417 Potters Ave. Scotti, OR	85900-7850	7417 Potter Ave. Scotti, OR	85900-7850	Ⓐ Ⓑ Ⓒ Ⓓ
43	427 Overons Ave. Tulsa, OH	08373-3697	427 Overon Ave. Tulsa, OH	08373-3667	Ⓐ Ⓑ Ⓒ Ⓓ
44	165 Square St. Durham, MN	89358	1165 Square St. Durham, MN	89350	Ⓐ Ⓑ Ⓒ Ⓓ
45	853 Queens Rd. Laredo, MD	30331-4590	853 Queens Rd. Lareto, MD	30331-4290	Ⓐ Ⓑ Ⓒ Ⓓ

Address Checking Practice Test 3 (cont'd): Continue to compare each pair of addresses for errors and mark the answer sheet as follows:

A. No Errors   **B.** Address Only   **C.** Zip Code Only   **D.** Both Address and ZIP Code

	Correct List of Addresses		Address List to be Checked		
	Address	**ZIP**	**Address**	**ZIP**	**Answer Grid**
46	4837 Holder Rd. Chandler, PA	55673	4837 Holder Rd. Chandler, PA	55673	Ⓐ Ⓑ Ⓒ Ⓓ
47	1743 Broad Street Glendale, KS	96869	1743 Broad Street Glendale, KS	96866	Ⓐ Ⓑ Ⓒ Ⓓ
48	3561 Thunder St. Plano, MD	24212-7372	356 Thunder Zt. Plano, MD	24212-7372	Ⓐ Ⓑ Ⓒ Ⓓ
49	172 Waller Ave. Lincoln, WA	60435	172 Wall Ave. Lincoln, WA	60432	Ⓐ Ⓑ Ⓒ Ⓓ
50	8282 Young St. Buffalo, MS	33890-3322	8282 Young St. Buffalo, MS	33890-3322	Ⓐ Ⓑ Ⓒ Ⓓ
51	4171 Sheps Way Austin, FL	46516	4171 Shepps Way Austin, FL	46516	Ⓐ Ⓑ Ⓒ Ⓓ
52	2922 Bancor St. Henderson, MJ	54438-1113	2922 Bancor St. Henderson, MJ	54438-1113	Ⓐ Ⓑ Ⓒ Ⓓ
53	667 Springer Way Raleigh, AK	37916-3896	667 Springer Way Raleigh, AK	37916-3894	Ⓐ Ⓑ Ⓒ Ⓓ
54	5182 Trader Ave. Memphis, MO	15226-3285	5182 Traker Ave. Memphis, MO	15526-3285	Ⓐ Ⓑ Ⓒ Ⓓ
55	2583 Election Ln. Tempo, VA	69859	2583 Election Ln. Tempo, VA	66859	Ⓐ Ⓑ Ⓒ Ⓓ
56	176 Numeral Ct. Aurora, RI	69457	1716 Numeral Ct. Aurora, RI	69457	Ⓐ Ⓑ Ⓒ Ⓓ
57	4896 Rastern St. Riverside, IL	21107-4724	489 Rastern St. Riverside, IL	27107-4724	Ⓐ Ⓑ Ⓒ Ⓓ
58	921 Soldiers Rd. Columbus, AR	14814	92 Soldiers Rd. Columbus, AR	14874	Ⓐ Ⓑ Ⓒ Ⓓ
59	3374 Happer Ln. El Paso, CA	16403	3374 Happer Ln. El Paso, CA	16403	Ⓐ Ⓑ Ⓒ Ⓓ
60	P.O. Box 1208 Toledo, IL	27071-6755	P.O. Box 1203 Toledo, IL	27071-6755	Ⓐ Ⓑ Ⓒ Ⓓ

Forms Completion Practice Test 3

This part of the test consists of 5 different forms and 30 questions relating to the 5 forms. Study each form and then answer the questions following each of the forms. (Time allowed: 15 minutes for 30 questions).

Answer questions 1 – 6 based on the following form:

RECEIPT FOR REGISTERED MAIL		
1. This section is to be completed by the post office.	2. Registered Number:	4. Date Stamp
	3. Registration Fee $ _____	5. Charge for Handling / 8. Fee for Return Receipt
		6. Postage Amount / 9. Fee for Restricted Delivery
		7. Received by
10. This section is to be completed by the postal customer. **Please PRINT with ballpoint pen, or TYPE.**	11. TO:	
	12. FROM:	

FORM # 7477 (Copy 1 – Customer) (Copy 2 – Post Office)

(See information on reverse side of this form.)

	Question	Answer Grid
1	The fee for Return Receipt should be entered in which box? A. 3 B. 7 C. 8 D. 2	Ⓐ Ⓑ Ⓒ Ⓓ
2	Which of the following boxes should not be completed by the post office? A. 5 B. 7 C. 6 D. 12	Ⓐ Ⓑ Ⓒ Ⓓ
3	Where on this form should the customer enter his name and address? A. 7 B. 11 C. 12 D. 4	Ⓐ Ⓑ Ⓒ Ⓓ
4	Which of the following is a correct entry for box 3? A. done B. 9/12/10 C. 6.50 D. 9:13	Ⓐ Ⓑ Ⓒ Ⓓ
5	The customer paid $16.00 charge for handling. This amount should be recorded in which box? A. 2 B. 5 C. 7 D. 12	Ⓐ Ⓑ Ⓒ Ⓓ
6	In which box should the Registered Number be entered? A. 5 B. 9 C. 8 D. 2	Ⓐ Ⓑ Ⓒ Ⓓ

(Answers for Test 3 are on page 122.)

Answer questions 7 – 12 based on the following form:

1. RECEIPT FOR INSURED MAIL		
15.	2. Postage	6. ☐ Fragile 7. ☐ Perishable
		8. ☐ Liquid 9. ☐ Hazardous
	3. Insurance Fee	10.
		11. Stamp Postmark Here
	4. Handling Fee	
	5. Total (Postage plus Fees) $_____	
12. Addressee (Sent to):		
13. Street, Apt. Number; or PO Box Number		
14. City, State and ZIP		

Question	Answer Grid
7 The first and last name of the addressee should be entered in box: A. 14 B. 13 C. 9 D. 12	Ⓐ Ⓑ Ⓒ Ⓓ
8 The postmark should be stamped in which box? A. 8 B. 10 C. 11 D. 15	Ⓐ Ⓑ Ⓒ Ⓓ
9 The State of the Addressee should be entered in which box? A. 14 B. 13 C. 12 D. 15	Ⓐ Ⓑ Ⓒ Ⓓ
10 Which of the following is a correct entry for box 4? A. 8/11 B. 9/1/10 C. $3.25 D. CM	Ⓐ Ⓑ Ⓒ Ⓓ
11 The contents of the article is a glass bottle. Which box should be checked? A. 6 B. 7 C. 8 D. 9	Ⓐ Ⓑ Ⓒ Ⓓ
12 The postage is $4.25. This should be entered in which box? A. 4 B. 3 C. 2 D. 11	Ⓐ Ⓑ Ⓒ Ⓓ

(Answers for Test 3 are on page 122.)

Answer questions 13 – 18 based on the following form:

CUSTOMS DECLARATION	
FROM (SENDER): 1. Last and First Name (and Business Name, if any) 2. Street 3. City 4. State 5. Zip	11. Insured Amount
	12. Insured Fees (U.S. $)
	13. Importer's Name and Telephone Number

TO (ADDRESSEE):
 	
6. Last and First Name (and Business Name, if any)
 	
7. Street
 	
8. City
 	
9. State   10. Zip
	14. Sender's instructions in case cannot be delivered:
	15. □ Treat as abandoned
	   □ Return to sender
	   □ Redirect to following address (#16):
	16.

17. Specific description of contents	18. Qty	19. Lbs.	20. Oz.
21. Comments			
22. Check one 23. □ Airmail/Priority 24. □ Surface/Non priority			
25. Check one 26. □ Documents 27. □ Merchandise 28. □ Gift 29. □ Other _____			
30. Date Signed 31. Sender's Signature			

	Question	Answer Grid
13	The Insured Amount is $300.00 and the Insured Fees are $9.75. Which amount should be entered in box 12? A. 309.75 B. 9.75 C. 300.00 D. 39	Ⓐ Ⓑ Ⓒ Ⓓ
14	The contents should be specifically described in which box? A. 16 B. 21 C. 17 D. 25	Ⓐ Ⓑ Ⓒ Ⓓ
15	Where on this form should the customer sign? A. 1 B. 29 C. 6 D. 31	Ⓐ Ⓑ Ⓒ Ⓓ
16	Which of the following is a correct entry for box 30? A. done B. 9/12/10 C. March D. N/A	Ⓐ Ⓑ Ⓒ Ⓓ
17	If the article cannot be delivered, the customer wishes that it be returned to him. To convey this, the customer must check off the appropriate box in section: A. 27 B. 15 C. 24 D. 26	Ⓐ Ⓑ Ⓒ Ⓓ
18	The sender signs the customs declaration on 7/25/10. In which box should this date be indicated? A. 1 B. 30 C. 10 D. 11	Ⓐ Ⓑ Ⓒ Ⓓ

(Answers for Test 3 are on page 122.)

Answer questions 19 – 24 based on the following form:

HOLD MAIL (AUTHORIZATION)		
1. This form authorizes the USPS to hold mail for a minimum of 3 days but not more than 30 days for the following individual(s).		
2. Name(s)		
3. Address (including number and street, Apartment or suite number, city, state, ZIP)		
4. A. □ I shall pick up my mail upon my return. I understand that if I do not pick up my mail, then mail delivery will not be made until I pick up the mail.		
4.B. □ I am authorizing the USPS to deliver all held mail and resume mail delivery on the end ing date indicated below.		
5. Beginning Date To Hold Mail	6. Ending Date To Hold Mail (This date can only be changed by the customer – in writing)	7. Signature of Customer
Shaded section is for Post Office (USPS) use only.		
8. Date this form received:		
9. Carrier name and ID Number receiving this form:	10. Carrier Name	11. Carrier ID Number
12. Clerk name and ID Number receiving this form	13. Clerk Name	14. Clerk ID Number
15. If option B was selected, complete this section: 16. □ All mail has been picked up on (Date)_____ 17. □ Regular mail delivery to be resumed on (Date) _____		
Signature of: 18. USPS Employee: _____19. Date Signed: _____		

	Question	Answer Grid
19	Which of the following boxes is not to be completed by the customer? A. 10 B. 5 C. 3 D. 2	Ⓐ Ⓑ Ⓒ Ⓓ
20	The customer signs in which box? A. 18 B. 7 C. 2 D. 10	Ⓐ Ⓑ Ⓒ Ⓓ
21	Where on this form should the clerk or carrier sign? A. 2 B. 7 C. 18 D. 19	Ⓐ Ⓑ Ⓒ Ⓓ
22	Which of the following is a correct entry for box 6? A. done B. 6/1/10 C. $6.50 D. 1	Ⓐ Ⓑ Ⓒ Ⓓ
23	This form authorizes the USPS to hold mail for a maximum of how many days? A. 13 B. 13 C. 33 D. 30	Ⓐ Ⓑ Ⓒ Ⓓ
24	If a clerk receives this form, the clerk's I.D. number must be entered in which box? A. 11 B. 7 C. 14 D. 19	Ⓐ Ⓑ Ⓒ Ⓓ

(Answers for Test 3 are on page 122.)

Answer questions 25 – 30 based on the following form:

Application for Nonprofit Standard Mail Prices	
1. Legal Name of Organization	2. Street Address (including Street/Suite Number)
	3. City, State, Zip
4. Telephone	5. E-mail address
6. Alternate mailing address (if any)	
Type of Organization (Check only one box) 7. □ Educational 8. □ Religious 9. □ Scientific 10. □ Labor 11. □ Veterans	
12. Has this organization previously mailed at nonprofit standard prices? 13. □ YES 14. □ NO	15. If the answer to 12 is "YES", have standard mail privileges ever been revoked? 16. □ YES 17. □ NO
18. Signature of applicant	19. Title of applicant
20. Date this request is submitted.	21.

	Question	Answer Grid
25	The telephone number of the organization is entered in which box? A. 1 B. 2 C. 3 D. 4	Ⓐ Ⓑ Ⓒ Ⓓ
26	The applicant signs in which box? A. 1 B. 19 C. 18 D. 20	Ⓐ Ⓑ Ⓒ Ⓓ

27	Where on this form should the date the request is submitted be entered? A. 7 B. 19 C. 20 D. 18	Ⓐ Ⓑ Ⓒ Ⓓ
28	Which of the following is a correct entry for box 19? A. done B. Pres. C. $6.50 D. $5	Ⓐ Ⓑ Ⓒ Ⓓ
29	The organization is a nonprofit Veterans organization. This is indicated by checking box: A. 8 B. 7 C. 9 D. 11	Ⓐ Ⓑ Ⓒ Ⓓ
30	The E-mail address of the organization should be entered in box: A. 1 B. 2 C. 3 D. 5	Ⓐ Ⓑ Ⓒ Ⓓ

(Answers for Test 3 are on page 122.)

Directions for the following 36 Coding Questions

For each of the following 36 "Delivery Addresses" determine based on the coding guide whether the address belongs to Delivery Route A, B, C or D, and mark your answer grid accordingly. You have 6 minutes to code the 36 addresses.

Coding Practice Test #3: Coding Guide

Range of Addresses	Delivery Route
50 – 600 London Lane 1 – 500 Condor Ave. 100 – 1200 N. 69th Street	A
601– 1200 London Lane 1201 - 2000 N. 69th Street	B
1000 – 1900 Gordon Ave. 200 – 1500 Patterson Circle 501 – 2000 Condor Ave.	C
All mail that doesn't fall in one of the address ranges listed above	D

	Delivery Address	Delivery Route				Answer Grid
1	500 London Lane	A	B	C	D	Ⓐ Ⓑ Ⓒ Ⓓ
2	1000 Gordon Ave.	A	B	C	D	Ⓐ Ⓑ Ⓒ Ⓓ
3	1 Condor Ave.	A	B	C	D	Ⓐ Ⓑ Ⓒ Ⓓ
4	610 London Lane	A	B	C	D	Ⓐ Ⓑ Ⓒ Ⓓ
5	3000 Condor Ave.	A	B	C	D	Ⓐ Ⓑ Ⓒ Ⓓ
6	700 N. 69th Street	A	B	C	D	Ⓐ Ⓑ Ⓒ Ⓓ
7	1901 N. 69th Street	A	B	C	D	Ⓐ Ⓑ Ⓒ Ⓓ
8	2000 Gordon Ave.	A	B	C	D	Ⓐ Ⓑ Ⓒ Ⓓ
9	425 London Lane	A	B	C	D	Ⓐ Ⓑ Ⓒ Ⓓ
10	690 Condor Ave.	A	B	C	D	Ⓐ Ⓑ Ⓒ Ⓓ
11	200 Patterson Circle	A	B	C	D	Ⓐ Ⓑ Ⓒ Ⓓ
12	1100 N. 69th Street	A	B	C	D	Ⓐ Ⓑ Ⓒ Ⓓ
13	1249 Gordon Ave.	A	B	C	D	Ⓐ Ⓑ Ⓒ Ⓓ
14	469 Condor Ave.	A	B	C	D	Ⓐ Ⓑ Ⓒ Ⓓ

	Delivery Address	Delivery Route				Answer Grid
15	1500 Patterson Circle	A	B	C	D	Ⓐ Ⓑ Ⓒ Ⓓ
16	600 London Lane	A	B	C	D	Ⓐ Ⓑ Ⓒ Ⓓ
17	1585 N. 69th Street	A	B	C	D	Ⓐ Ⓑ Ⓒ Ⓓ
18	860 London Lane	A	B	C	D	Ⓐ Ⓑ Ⓒ Ⓓ
19	1000 Billings Way	A	B	C	D	Ⓐ Ⓑ Ⓒ Ⓓ
20	125 Condor Ave.	A	B	C	D	Ⓐ Ⓑ Ⓒ Ⓓ
21	1340 Gordon Ave.	A	B	C	D	Ⓐ Ⓑ Ⓒ Ⓓ
22	3247 Gordon Ave.	A	B	C	D	Ⓐ Ⓑ Ⓒ Ⓓ
23	625 N. 69th Street	A	B	C	D	Ⓐ Ⓑ Ⓒ Ⓓ
24	907 Condor Ave.	A	B	C	D	Ⓐ Ⓑ Ⓒ Ⓓ
25	1678 Ridge Pkwy.	A	B	C	D	Ⓐ Ⓑ Ⓒ Ⓓ
26	987 London Lane	A	B	C	D	Ⓐ Ⓑ Ⓒ Ⓓ
27	459 Patterson Circle	A	B	C	D	Ⓐ Ⓑ Ⓒ Ⓓ
28	1290 Gordon Ave.	A	B	C	D	Ⓐ Ⓑ Ⓒ Ⓓ
29	4956 Hartman Road	A	B	C	D	Ⓐ Ⓑ Ⓒ Ⓓ
30	411 Condor Ave.	A	B	C	D	Ⓐ Ⓑ Ⓒ Ⓓ
31	1357 Condor Ave.	A	B	C	D	Ⓐ Ⓑ Ⓒ Ⓓ
32	1050 London Lane	A	B	C	D	Ⓐ Ⓑ Ⓒ Ⓓ
33	1777 N. 69th Street	A	B	C	D	Ⓐ Ⓑ Ⓒ Ⓓ
34	335 London Lane	A	B	C	D	Ⓐ Ⓑ Ⓒ Ⓓ
35	1200 Patterson Circle	A	B	C	D	Ⓐ Ⓑ Ⓒ Ⓓ
36	879 N. 69th Street	A	B	C	D	Ⓐ Ⓑ Ⓒ Ⓓ

Memory Practice Test #3:   Coding Guide

Range of Addresses	Delivery Route
You have 5 minutes to memorize the Coding Guide on page 118, then code the following 36 addresses based on your <u>memory</u> of the coding guide. **(On the actual test you will probably have several minutes to practice answering coding questions. Those minutes can also be used, if you wish, to further memorize the codes.)** **You have 7 minutes to answer the following 36 coding questions**.	

	Delivery Address	Delivery Route				Answer Grid
1	125 Condor Ave.	A	B	C	D	Ⓐ Ⓑ Ⓒ Ⓓ
2	609 London Lane	A	B	C	D	Ⓐ Ⓑ Ⓒ Ⓓ
3	1000 N. 69th Street	A	B	C	D	Ⓐ Ⓑ Ⓒ Ⓓ
4	9000 Condor Ave.	A	B	C	D	Ⓐ Ⓑ Ⓒ Ⓓ
5	1100 Gordon Ave.	A	B	C	D	Ⓐ Ⓑ Ⓒ Ⓓ
6	334 Condor Ave.	A	B	C	D	Ⓐ Ⓑ Ⓒ Ⓓ
7	1500 Patterson Circle	A	B	C	D	Ⓐ Ⓑ Ⓒ Ⓓ
8	860 London Lane	A	B	C	D	Ⓐ Ⓑ Ⓒ Ⓓ
9	1290 N. 69th Street	A	B	C	D	Ⓐ Ⓑ Ⓒ Ⓓ
10	907 Condor Ave.	A	B	C	D	Ⓐ Ⓑ Ⓒ Ⓓ
11	997 N. 69th Street	A	B	C	D	Ⓐ Ⓑ Ⓒ Ⓓ
12	876 Neiman Place	A	B	C	D	Ⓐ Ⓑ Ⓒ Ⓓ
13	50 London Lane	A	B	C	D	Ⓐ Ⓑ Ⓒ Ⓓ
14	1556 Gordon Ave.	A	B	C	D	Ⓐ Ⓑ Ⓒ Ⓓ

	Delivery Address	Delivery Route				Answer Grid
15	100 N. 69th Street	A	B	C	D	Ⓐ Ⓑ Ⓒ Ⓓ
16	1720 N. 69th Street	A	B	C	D	Ⓐ Ⓑ Ⓒ Ⓓ
17	2500 Patterson Circle	A	B	C	D	Ⓐ Ⓑ Ⓒ Ⓓ
18	500 London Lane	A	B	C	D	Ⓐ Ⓑ Ⓒ Ⓓ
19	1444 Condor Ave.	A	B	C	D	Ⓐ Ⓑ Ⓒ Ⓓ
20	245 Patterson Circle	A	B	C	D	Ⓐ Ⓑ Ⓒ Ⓓ
21	245 Condor Ave.	A	B	C	D	Ⓐ Ⓑ Ⓒ Ⓓ
22	1648 Gordon Ave.	A	B	C	D	Ⓐ Ⓑ Ⓒ Ⓓ
23	933 Fuller Street	A	B	C	D	Ⓐ Ⓑ Ⓒ Ⓓ
24	1500 N. 69th Street	A	B	C	D	Ⓐ Ⓑ Ⓒ Ⓓ
25	450 London Lane	A	B	C	D	Ⓐ Ⓑ Ⓒ Ⓓ
26	200 Peterson Circle	A	B	C	D	Ⓐ Ⓑ Ⓒ Ⓓ
27	955 London Lane	A	B	C	D	Ⓐ Ⓑ Ⓒ Ⓓ
28	1900 Gordon Ave.	A	B	C	D	Ⓐ Ⓑ Ⓒ Ⓓ
29	1550 Patterson Circle	A	B	C	D	Ⓐ Ⓑ Ⓒ Ⓓ
30	1100 N. 69th Street	A	B	C	D	Ⓐ Ⓑ Ⓒ Ⓓ
31	769 London Lane	A	B	C	D	Ⓐ Ⓑ Ⓒ Ⓓ
32	1200 Patterson Circle	A	B	C	D	Ⓐ Ⓑ Ⓒ Ⓓ
33	477 London Lane	A	B	C	D	Ⓐ Ⓑ Ⓒ Ⓓ
34	2000 Condor Ave.	A	B	C	D	Ⓐ Ⓑ Ⓒ Ⓓ
35	1775 N. 69th Street	A	B	C	D	Ⓐ Ⓑ Ⓒ Ⓓ
36	465 Condor Ave.	A	B	C	D	Ⓐ Ⓑ Ⓒ Ⓓ

Answers: Practice Test #3

Address Checking

1. B	7. B	13. B	19. A	25. A	31. B	37. C	43. D	49. D	55. C
2. B	8. D	14. D	20. D	26. B	32. C	38. A	44. D	50. A	56. B
3. C	9. A	15. C	21. B	27. D	33. D	39. D	45. D	51. B	57. D
4. D	10. C	16. A	22. C	28. A	34. D	40. C	46. A	52. A	58. D
5. A	11. B	17. B	23. C	29. D	35. A	41. A	47. C	53. C	59. A
6. C	12. D	18. A	24. D	30. B	36. B	42. B	48. B	54. D	60. B

Forms Completion

1. C	6. D	11. A	16. B	21. C	26. C
2. D	7. D	12. C	17. B	22. B	27. C
3. C	8. C	13. B	18. B	23. D	28. B
4. C	9. A	14. C	19. A	24. C	29. D
5. B	10. C	15. D	20. B	25. D	30. D

Coding

1. A	5. D	9. A	13. C	17. B	21. C	25. D	29. D	33. B
2. C	6. A	10. C	14. A	18. B	22. D	26. B	30. A	34. A
3. A	7. B	11. C	15. C	19. D	23. A	27. C	31. C	35. C
4. B	8. D	12. A	16. A	20. A	24. C	28. C	32. B	36. A

Memory

1. A	5. C	9. B	13. A	17. D	21. A	25. A	29. D	33. A
2. B	6. A	10. C	14. C	18. A	22. C	26. D	30. A	34. C
3. A	7. C	11. A	15. A	19. C	23. D	27. B	31. B	35. B
4. D	8. B	12. D	16. B	20. C	24. B	28. C	32. C	36. A

For the FREE samples of the questions online, please visit:

www.PostalTest.com

(For FREE INTERACTIVE Access Code, see Page 63)

<u>Good luck!</u>

<u>Notes</u>

CPSIA information can be obtained
at www.ICGtesting.com
Printed in the USA
LVOW09s0214100518
576678LV00019B/637/P